PEOPLE & PATTERNS

THE CARPET WEAVING INDUSTRY
IN 19TH CENTURY BARNARD CASTLE

Edited by

Denis Coggins

Published by

The Friends of The Bowes Museum

Published by the Friends of The Bowes Museum with help
from the Marc Fitch Fund and Durham County Council in
conjunction with the exhibition

PEOPLE & PATTERNS
THE CARPET WEAVING INDUSTRY
IN 19TH CENTURY BARNARD CASTLE

21 SEPTEMBER 1996 -
5 JANUARY 1997

THE BOWES MUSEUM
BARNARD CASTLE, CO. DURHAM

Designed by: Blue the design company

Printed by: G. W. Belton Ltd.

ISBN 0-9508165-1-5

Front cover: see plate 13
Back cover: see plate 5

Arts, Libraries & Museums Department

CONTENTS

Acknowledgements

Notes on contributors

Introduction   Sarah Medlam

Chapter   1   Barnard Castle and the carpet trade   Sarah Medlam and
                                                                Denis Coggins

             2   Fashions in carpeting   Joanna Hashagen

             3   The carpets of Barnard Castle   Joanna Hashagen

             4   Carpet manufacturers in Barnard Castle   Jean Hemingway

             5   Industrial premises   Jean Hemingway

             6   The workforce   Jean Hemingway

             7   Jacob Allison: a case study   Jean Hemingway

             8   Living conditions   Alan Wilkinson

             9   Then and now: the visible evidence   Alan Wilkinson

Catalogue of carpets   Joanna Hashagen

Appendix I   The kinds of wool used in the
              manufacture of carpets   Michael L. Ryder

Appendix II   Dye analysis of wool samples   G. W. Taylor

List of known carpet manufacturers

Designs registered in the Public Record Office

Glossary

Bibliography

ACKNOWLEDGMENTS

This book and the exhibition which it accompanies, have been made possible by the efforts of very many people. Our thanks must first go to the Friends of The Bowes Museum whose generous financial help has enabled this book to be published, with the help of a substantial grant from the Marc Fitch Fund. Further financial assistance has been provided by Durham County Council, who also funded the exhibition as part of Visual Arts Year, 1996. The Pasold Research Fund provided a grant towards the technical analysis of the carpets.

We wish to thank the lenders who went to great trouble to facilitate their loans: Lord Barnard, John Chichester Constable, John Claridge, Mrs. M. Hamilton, Wendy Hefford, The National Trust, and the Rector and Church wardens of St. Mary's Church, Staindrop. Valuable help was also given by those who gave permission to record existing buildings: Mrs. H. Barker, Mrs. K. Bowman, Mr. M. Fryer.

We are grateful to those who gave permission to publish photographs and they are credited under their illustrations. All other photographs are from the The Bowes Museum collections. Some were taken by Syd Neville especially for the book. The designs in the P. R. O. were photographed by Cliff Birtchnell.

For technical help we are grateful to The University of Huddersfield, especially Catherine Atkinson, Alan Buck and Roger Hallos, the students Jennifer McClory, Kirsty Nicholson, Angela Valorose. Anna Benson and Neil Warburton, Mary and Michael Crompton, Caroline Rendell, and Penelope Walton Rogers, kindly gave specialist advice.

Museum staff, especially Margaret Eggleston, Dinah Jones and Syd Neville have worked tirelessly on the project. Volunteers who have given invaluable time include members of the South Durham and North Yorkshire Branch of N.A.D.F.A.S. organised by Sue Longridge, and Museum volunteers Margaret Harley, Bridget Westmacott and Joyce Williams.

Many local people have provided information including: Miss Dunn, Mr. R. Jackson, Mr. R. Johnson, Brian Kent, Frank Little, Mr. Littlefair, Mrs. Nixon, Mr. and Mrs. Pounder, Parkin Raine, Elizabeth Steele and David Hall of Raby Castle, Mr. Sutcliffe, and the late Mr. J.C. Walker.

We are also indebted to those further afield who have provided specific information: Linda Baumgarten of the Colonial Williamsburg Foundation, David Butler and Jennifer Gill of D.C.R.O., the staff of the Borthwick Institute, David Connell of Burton Constable, the staff of the Centre for Local Studies in Darlington Public Library, Durham University Department of Paleography, Mr. A. G. Morison, Company Secretary of Hays plc, Mr. Barbour of Hugh Mackay Carpets.

Colleagues, including John Cornforth, Christopher Gilbert, Ian Gow, Wendy Hefford, Sarah Sherrill and Margaret Swain have encouraged and advised on the project from the beginning. Many other people have given support, especially Nick Hashagen and Michael Hemingway. We are grateful to them all. The continued interest of those who have been involved has encouraged us to produce this account of a brief but important episode in the industrial history of Barnard Castle.

Denis Coggins is a native of upper Teesdale and has studied its archaeology and history for many years. He was lecturer in history and archaeology at Middleton St. George College of Education between 1970 and 1979. From 1978 to 1988 he was Antiquities Officer at The Bowes Museum, Barnard Castle.

Joanna Hashagen is Costume and Textiles Officer at The Bowes Museum. Before this she was Assistant Keeper at the Gallery of English Costume, Manchester from 1977 to 1981. For the last fifteen years she has been working on the large and wide-ranging collections of textiles at The Bowes Museum. She has published articles on various aspects of the collection and curated a number of exhibitions including French Chair Covers of the 17th and 18th Centuries, Royal Style and People and Patterns.

Jean Hemingway gained an M.A. (Education) Degree, specialising in research methods, from the University of Lancaster. She has been privileged to investigate the manuscript accounts of Jacob Allison (fl. 1825-1840), and has been researching the personal and economic history of the carpet manufacturers in Barnard Castle during the nineteenth century.

Sarah Medlam was Furniture Officer at The Bowes Museum from 1974 until 1992, when she moved to be Deputy Curator of the Department of Furniture and Woodwork at the Victoria & Albert Museum in London. From 1992-5 she was the editor of the journal Furniture History. While at The Bowes Museum she gathered much basic material on the carpet trade in the town, her interest spurred by the discovery of a flat-woven carpet used as an underfelt in her rented cottage (Cat. No. 7 presented by its owners to The Bowes Museum).

Dr. M.L. Ryder is a former researcher of animal fibres. He is a biology graduate of Leeds University, but took his research degrees in the Textile Department and began his career at the then Wool Industries Research Association. He spent three years as Senior Lecturer in Wool in an Australian university and then twenty-five years in Edinburgh, first at the Animal Breeding Research Organisation and latterly at the Hill Farming Research Organisation. He is now an independent author and natural fibre consultant concentrating on archaeological material.

Dr. G.W. Taylor obtained his PhD in Chemistry at Cambridge University and then worked as a Research Manager in the Fibres Division of I.C.I. Since taking early retirement from I.C.I. he has worked on the identification of dyes in early textiles with Textile Research Associates, York.

Alan Wilkinson graduated in English Language and Literature at Oxford University before teaching in North Wales and, for thirty-six years, at Barnard Castle School where he retired as Head of English in 1988. A native of the town, he has studied the history of Barnard Castle for many years. His publications include Barnard Castle in old picture postcards, in two volumes (European Library, 1983 and 1990).

INTRODUCTION

Barnard Castle's reputation as a tourist centre developed so steadily during the nineteenth century and has become so accepted in the twentieth that it is easy to forget that during most of this time the picturesque and the industrial existed side-by-side in Teesdale. During the first half of the nineteenth century, indeed, the town saw the development of a whole new industry, that of carpet-weaving. By the time of the 1851 census 365 people out of a total recorded population of 4,608 in the town were employed in several factories which manufactured carpets (see Chapter 6). Yet within twenty years this specialized trade was in serious decline and by the turn of the century the last carpet factory had closed.

Apart from an article in the local paper, the *Teesdale Mercury* (17 December 1930) by Sidney Harrison, the then curator of The Bowes Museum, little systematic effort was made to record the industry. Most reference to it was confined to anecdote, to mention in late nineteenth century obituaries of those connected with the trade, and to quotations from general local histories and trade directories of the nineteenth century. It seemed to be accepted, even by the 1930s, that very little had survived of the architecture of the industry and even less of its records or products.

Indeed, the very term 'carpet' was confusing, conjuring up a modern image of thick piled floor-covering, very different form the flat-woven woollen carpets (not unlike the modern 'Welsh tapestry' used for bedspreads and bags) which were used in a wide range of Victorian households (see Chapter 2). Even within the town, these carpets would not, by the time of the Second World War, have been recognized as such by the grandchildren and great-grandchildren of those who had spent their lives making them and all too many of them had by then probably been put on the bonfire as hopelessly old-fashioned, if not entirely worn out.

During the 1950s even more of the architectural evidence for the industry was lost in the re-development of Bridgegate (see Chapter 9). The chances of ever properly recording this aspect of Barnard Castle's history seemed remote. There were some very important documentary sources which had always been known, in particular the *Report to the General Board of Health* by W. Ranger, published in 1850 after an outbreak of cholera swept through the poorer areas of the town. This was an eloquent record of the squalor of the weavers' living conditions (see Chapter 8). Some of the standard sources for historians (census returns, parish records, local newspapers, local archives) could yield useful statistical material, but real hope of knowing more of what the carpets looked like, their design and their colour, did not come until two important discoveries were made.

In 1987 Ian Gow, of the Royal Commission on the Ancient and Historical Monuments of Scotland, working in the Public Record Office at Kew, came across a group of designs for carpets registered by Barnard Castle firms between 1842 and 1853 (see Chapter 3). He passed the information to me at The Bowes Museum and after a thorough search of the design registers the designs have now been photographed for the exhibition.

Even more recent is the discovery of a crucially important group of day-books and cash-books belonging to one of the earliest firms, that of Jacob Allison (see Chapter 7). These books, at first glance a dry compendium of columns of figures and lists of addresses, with thorough study and analysis undertaken specially for this exhibition by Jean Hemingway, have provided us with a remarkably clear view of how a carpet business was conducted in Barnard Castle in the years before the railway came to the town, and even of such details as the colours which were popular in the 1820s and 1830s and where such carpets were sold and who might have been covering their floors with the products of Barnard Castle.

These discoveries were enormously encouraging and at last an exhibition seemed possible. Exhibitions and books, however, do not appear by magic: the many discoveries recorded here are the result of months of detailed and careful work by several people with differing but overlapping interests in the subject. Groups of volunteers willingly undertook the essential but tedious task of checking such sources as the local newspapers. For too long the history of the industry had relied on anecdote and vague tradition and it is pleasing to discover, for instance, a secure date for the building of Thorngate Mill, one of the most important surviving buildings of the industry. The notes and papers associated with work on the exhibition will all be lodged in The Bowes Museum for the benefit of future researchers in the subject, including an index of all people known to have been associated with the industry (compiled from census returns, parish records and other sources) - an important tool also for those who are working on family history in Teesdale.

The tradition of carpet weaving in Co. Durham is continued by the Durham City firm of Hugh Mackay. The father of the original Hugh Mackay started his life as a weaver in Barnard Castle (signing a statement on the working conditions of the weavers quoted in Ranger's report in 1850). It is thus pleasing that the firm of Hugh Mackay are using one of the designs registered by Pratt & Co (fig. 20) as the basis of a design for a new staircarpet for The Bowes Museum.

Most pleasing of all has been the discovery of several more carpets or fragments of carpets, and the catalogue at the end of the book lists all known pieces which can be securely, or by circumstantial evidence, attributed to the Barnard Castle factories. Previous appeals through local newspapers had brought to light certain pieces of information, but is is only the sustained work for this exhibition that has unearthed the carpets themselves, rare survivals and documents of this industry which once dominated the town.

The subject unites both sides of The Bowes Museum's interests, the decorative arts and local history and it is fitting in Visual Arts Year in the North-East that Barnard Castle's unique contribution to the decorative arts in Britain should be celebrated.

Sarah Medlam.

Notes to the Text

The book has been organised so that it can be read by both the general reader and the specialist. The nine chapters tell the story of the industry. The detailed results of the research and technical analysis are provided in the appendices and in a catalogue of carpets shown in the exhibition. The book ends with a glossary as there are, inevitably, some specialist terms within the main text. Full references for authors cited in the text are listed in the bibliography

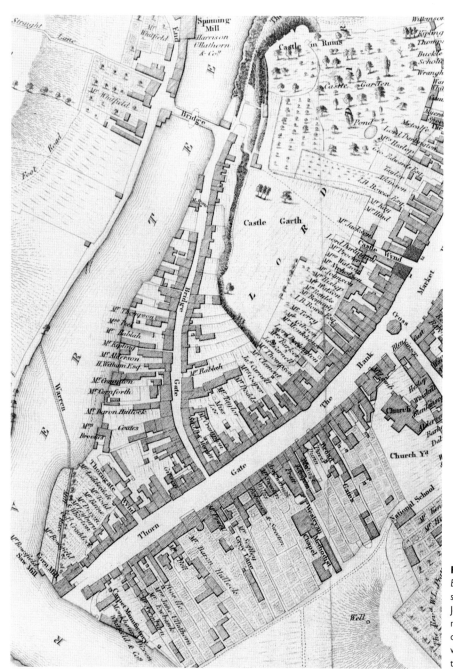

Fig. 1. Detail of a *Plan of Barnard Castle from actual survey,* 1827, published by John Wood. Many of the names are of the owners of the land, several of whom were leasing sites to carpet manufacturers.

BARNARD CASTLE AND THE CARPET TRADE

Historically, Barnard Castle had always supported itself with industries and trade related to the agricultural and mineral products of the dale, so the development of the carpet industry in the nineteenth century was a based on a long tradition. The town was founded as an adjunct of the castle whose name it shares, which was begun in about 1095 by Guy de Balliol who had been given the estates of Gainford and Middleton in Teesdale by King William II. The gift was probably part of the King's plan to create a series of strong points commanding the Pennine dales (Kapelle, 1979, 148). Balliol moved the administrative centre of his estates from Gainford, choosing instead a site over-looking the ford where the Roman road between Bowes and Binchester forts crossed the river Tees. His nephew Bernard began in about 1135 to transform what had been a largely timber structure into one of the largest castles in the North and to create a new town beside it (fig. 2). The close connection between town and castle can be seen in the way that its three original streets; Galgate, Market and Thorngate follow the lines of the castle walls, as also does Bridgegate (fig. 1), constructed perhaps in the fourteenth century when the Roman ford was replaced by a bridge further down-stream (Austin, 1979, 9). The new town was created specifically to attract trade, encourage industry and thus add

Fig. 2. This, one of the earliest pictures of the castle, was drawn by William Hutchinson in 1781 and engraved for Volume III of his *History of Durham,* 1794. It shows how well the Balliols chose the site for their new head-quarters on the cliff above the Tees.

to the lord's revenues. Its situation at an important river crossing and at the junction between the mainly pastoral upper dale and arable lower dale was ideal in this respect, especially as in addition it enjoyed the protection of a formidable castle (fig.2). One of Bernard Balliol's first acts was to grant the new town a charter based on one granted some years before to the new town of Richmond on the river Swale. The establishment of a market in the town enabled produce from both the Middleton and Gainford estates to be sold and exchanged, and provided a source for the raw materials - lead, iron, wool, hides - needed for manufacturing. The fast-flowing river Tees could be used to provide power for mills and forges. Little is known of the industrial life of the town during the medieval and Tudor periods, though it figures occasionally in the political events of the times. By the early seventeenth century Barnard Castle was important enough to be named as a place entitled to return two members - both burgesses - to Parliament and later in the century at least eight tradesmen were successful enough to issue trade tokens in their own names (Fordyce, 1856, 12). In 1698, however, the tanners, leather dressers and glovers of the town petitioned parliament to remove the tax on leather as '... their trades are very much decayed' (Hutchinson, 1794, 229).

During the eighteenth century the chief manufacturing industries of the town were connected with leather and wool. In 1769 Arthur Young recorded that Barnard Castle was 'chiefly of note for stockings and bridles' (Young, 1770, 283). Gradually the woollen trades became dominant, using the fleeces of moorland and lowland sheep from local farms, though by the end of the century they too were beginning to decline (Hutchinson, 1794, 229). Spinning and weaving were carried on on a domestic scale but were concentrated in Bridgegate and Thorngate (figs 1 & 3).

William Hutchinson (1732-1814), historian, topographer and solicitor, himself a native of the town, summarized its trade thus: 'the town is very populous, the number of souls being computed at four thousand, there being a great manufactory carried on here of woollen goods, tammies, shags, crapes and stockings. This place was in very early times famous for leather and at this day many wealthy tanners reside here ... it is one of the greatest corn markets in the north of England' (Hutchinson, 1776, 339-40).

Fig. 3. Early eighteenth century houses in Thorngate with the typical row of small windows under the eaves designed to admit as much light as possible to the weaving workshops in the uppermost storey.

A watercolour by Thomas Hearne (1744-1817) dated 1788, illustrates clearly two important aspects of the town at that time (plate 1). The medieval bridge and the romantic ruins of the castle which were much admired by this early tourist and seeker after the picturesque, are complemented by the view of the western-most houses of Bridgegate, which was to remain throughout the nineteenth century the centre of woollen weaving in the town, close to the river which was so important for preparation and dyeing of the wool (figs. 1 & 4).

A little earlier than Hearne's painting the river Tees had been responsible for a brief moment of notoriety for the town. The great flood of 1771, which caused enormous destruction along all the rivers of the North, proved to be an unexpected benefactor to one of the town's dyers. Though the bridge across the river was one of the few to survive, the river swept round its southern end flooding the cellars of a property which is now the White Swan Inn (fig. 4): '... a few pieces of tammies were in the dye kettle at the time ... when the operator not chusing [sic] to run the risk of dying himself decamped with the utmost celerity. After the torrent subsided they were discovered to have attained a colour beyond his most sanguine expectations.... The articles were sent to the London market and gave such satisfaction that orders were forwarded for a further supply' (Layton, 1823, 16-17). Unfortunately it proved impossible to recreate the magical effect wrought by the flood water though Barnard Castle products continued to be noted for their colours '... due to the superior water of the Tees ...' (Layton, ibid.). But the woollen trade was always precarious, subject to every boom and recession, a situation exacerbated by the small scale of individual enterprises. The ending of the Napoleonic wars and the increase in cotton manufacture led to a sharp and catastrophic decline in the demand for woollen cloth, while unemployment was increased by the return of discharged

Fig. 4. Engraving from *Views & Scenery of Barnard Castle* by Rock & Co., London, 1857 showing the carpet factories on the right, perched on the edge of the Tees. The building on the far right, with hanks of wool hanging out to dry, is that of Dunn & Co. On the left, next to the bridge, is the building that was said to have been flooded in 1771 (now the White Swan Inn).

export trade in carpeting from Britain rose from a value of £33,000 in 1807 to £180,000 in 1817, as markets in America and the colonies began to follow a fashion which had developed in Britain in the second half of the eighteenth century (Bartlett, 1978, 49-51).

The development of this specialization in the town was not wholly led by the market. Concern for the plight of the unemployed was high and in 1815 a group of philanthropic Methodist business-men in Barnard Castle decided to invest money to create the carpet manufactory of Monkhouse, Whitfield and Dixon. A poem published on the occasion of the Jubilee of the National School at Barnard Castle on 2 September 1864 looked back with praise for:

those pious, generous, noble-hearted men ... who
devised the means without a hope of gain
of giving full employment to those men
who, thro' the pressure of these hard, hard times
had been reduced to poverty and want -
they set up weaving looms and soon both peace
and plenty smiled upon this town again

A note to the poem identifies the men as Wm. Dixon, Ebenezer Monkhouse and Joshua Monkhouse.

These developments coincided with a change from small domestic workshops to purpose-built factories for the weaving of woollens. The first reference to a strike in the town had been in 1810 when Annie Harwood was granted five

soldiers. In 1820 it was reported that though Barnard Castle possessed one of the largest corn markets in England, 'the labouring classes are chiefly employed in the manufacture of Scotch camblets or tammies and in the tanning and stocking business ... of late year the woollen trade has greatly declined' (Brayby and Britton, 1820, 234-5). Some form of diversification was necessary and this was provided in Barnard Castle by a change to the production of carpets. Tradition ascribes the foundation of the carpet weaving industry in the town to one Thomas Crampton in the first decade of the nineteenth century, though little is known of him or his enterprise (Henderson, 1863, 236). By beginning to produce carpets the town was boarding a bandwagon: the shillings a week poor relief 'in consequence of her being deprived of her work as a weaver by the unlawful combination of weavers in the town ...'. (quoted more than a century later in the *Teesdale Mercury* 17 April 1935). Weaving in the town was now set upon an entirely new path though it did not immediately lead to 'peace and plenty' as the poem suggests. The export trade in carpeting levelled off between

Fig. 5. Pencil drawing by R. Harley (1848-50) of Thorngate, from the river. The gable of Monkhouses 1846 building can be seen centre-right with the 1847-8 building prominent on the left. This drawing formed the basis of an engraved billhead for Monkhouses (fig. 25). (Mr. Frank Atkinson).

1815 and 1840 (Bartlett, 1978, 49-51), so growth depended on sales in Britain, where competition was intense. In 1826 for example 'stagnation of trade and cessation of manufactures' was reported of Barnard Castle with 151 heads of families unemployed and another 110 only partly employed (Spencer, 1866 *Local Records of South Durham,* under 7 July, 1826). Rather more optimistically Garland in 1828 recorded 'several manufactories for Brussels and other carpets etc. having been recently established which if successfully conducted and encouraged will materially enhance the wealth and consequence of the place' (Garland, 1828, 40). Six years later the same author was able to write that the carpet factories 'have been for some years carried on and the various owners have furnished goods of such superior

quality as to be able to successfully compete with the first manufacturers of the kingdom' (Garland, 1834, 39-40).

During the 1830s and 1840s, despite individual business failures, carpet making steadily developed in the town, gradually dominating the weaving trades. In 1834 there were at least seven firms in business (Pigot & Co. *Directory,* 1834) (see Chapter 4). The leading firm of Monkhouse was sufficiently important to become a member of the Northern Association of Carpet Makers in 1838 (Henderson, 1863, 241) and in 1846-8 completed a major new factory building in the town (fig. 5). In 1851 the firm was an exhibitor at the Great Exhibition (fig.11).

Hearne (plate 1) recorded the town at the time when carpet weaving was about to develop. The wood-engraved illustration published by a local printer in the 1860s records it as the industry was in decline. The engraving shows a pair of leisured fishermen below the walls of the castle, which is romantically clad in ivy (fig. 6). These foreground elements were designed to appeal to the new tourists brought by the railway. But Victorian tourists were as much interested in Progress as in the Picturesque and just as other engravings of the time show such wonders as the local railway viaduct, so here the picturesque view includes the carpet factories and the large woollen mills which by that time lined the riverside beyond the bridge and provided the largest source of employment in the town. The almost wistfully romantic mood of both Hearne's water-colour and the engraving disguises the brisk and sometimes difficult business life which occupied the people of Barnard Castle.

From its beginnings in the early years of the century the carpet trade of Barnard Castle was selling to a wide market. The day-book of the firm of Allison's in the 1820s shows an extensive trade with London retailers (Chapter 7). Some raw materials had to be brought into the area from considerable distances. Dyes, for example, came largely from a specialist supplier in Kendal on the west side of the Pennines in Cumbria. Inland journeys were by cumbersome carriers' wagons which regularly traversed the cross-Pennine route between Kendal and Barnard Castle and between Barnard Castle and the towns of Darlington, Stockton and Newcastle to the east and north. At the port of Stockton carpets might be transferred to ship for the sea-route to London. Unfortunately for Barnard Castle the rapidly expanding railway network did not reach the town until 1856 though negotiations had been in progress since 1833, much of the delay being due to problems with the largest landowner in the area, the Duke of Cleveland.

By the time the railway had been built the carpet industry's brief period of success was almost over. The entry for the town in the *Post Office Directory* of 1858 includes this statement 'in the early part of the present century the carpet manufacture was introduced and formed the staple trade of the place. It has however much declined ... the staple trade is now the manufacture of flax thread for shoemakers'. Only one firm of carpet makers - Monkhouse Bros. - was listed as being in business (Kelly & Co, 1858), though in fact others were still trading. In 1863 Monkhouses closed and the local newspaper reported that '... a large part of our working population have been compelled to move to other parts of the Country in search of employment which is no longer to be had in the town' (*Teesdale Mercury*, 2 December 1863).

If details of the commencement of carpet making in Barnard Castle are lacking, so too are details of its ending. Its decline and final disappearance cannot be attributed to any one cause but rather to a combination of factors among which the following may be considered: financial problems, problems of family and inheritance, and problems of location. Most if not all companies were under-financed and had to pay out of profits or capital rather than loans for improvements in premises or machinery. This was not peculiar to the carpet industry or to Barnard Castle, for, writing of the early years of the industrial revolution, the economic historian Hutton comments that 'the typical firm was family owned and if extra capital was required it was provided by investors known to the family ... local banks rarely did more than offer cash advances against invoices' (Hutton, 1995, 117). It would for example have been almost impossible for Barnard Castle manufacturers to afford to install the new power looms which were available from about 1850 even if their premises had been suitable. The constant risk of fire added to financial problems. A serious fire at Harrison, Crosby, Dunn & Co's premises occurred on 7 December 1824 (Richardson, 1843, X, 302). It was still considered

Fig. 6. This engraving is by R.W. Atkinson a Barnard Castle printer and publisher of the *Teesdale Mercury*. It is undated but was probably made in the 1860s.

noteworthy nearly twenty years afterwards. It is difficult to over-estimate the effect of family circumstances on the welfare of the companies. The untimely deaths of men such as Richard Atkin and, particularly, John Pratt were disastrous to a small industry (see Chapter 4). The *Darlington & Stockton Times* reporting the death of John Pratt in the cholera epidemic of 1849 stated on Saturday 9 September

(fig. 7). Despite strenuous efforts by many of the professional men of the town and in particular of J.C. Monkhouse, son of Joshua, the railway did not arrive in Barnard Castle until 1856 and then the station was built at a distance of over a mile from the factories. In a wider context Barnard Castle carpet makers were remote from any cluster of similar manufacturers so that resources could not be shared.

that on Sunday 3 September 'Mr. Pratt was taken ill together with his eldest daughter ... and ere the sun was set on the same day they were both lifeless corpses'. At the time it was said Mr. Pratt employed 200-300 people and had not long taken over the firm after the death of his father. His children were young and his widow, who declined to act as executrix, was apparently illiterate. Other manufacturers, Edward Raine (1786-1867), Richard Dunn (1787-1871) and George Jordan (1793-1849 - another cholera victim), had no sons to succeed them and to provide an incentive for new investment. The Monkhouse family by contrast had several sons who, however, dispersed into other businesses soon after their father retired. The location of the industry on a narrow strip of land beside the river made expansion very difficult

Fig. 7. A composite photograph giving a panoramic view of the factory buildings along the river from Ullathorne's flax mill on the left beyond the bridge to Thorngate on the right. The photograph, by Elijah Yeoman, a professional photographer in the town, is undated but was probably taken about the turn of the century.

As a result of these and other problems the industry was in decline by the mid century; the largest firm, Monkhouse Brothers, closed in 1863 and Smith & Co., closed in 1888. This was, however, not quite the end of the story for Whellan's *Directory* of 1894 lists 'Smith Bros. Carpet Weavers, Bridgegate' while the admission registers for Barnard Castle Infants School list the occupation of parents up to 1896 at which date three were described as 'carpet weavers'.

Plate 1. Watercolour of Barnard Castle, 1788, by Thomas Hearne (1744-1817) Two important aspects of the history of the town are brought together in this picture. The medieval bridge and ruined castle are complemented by the domestic and industrial buildings at the western end of Bridgegate, the centre of the woollen industry in the town.

Plate 2. Lithograph of the Long Gallery, Burton Constable, Hull, 1836-9, fitted with a triplecloth Kidderminster carpet which is still in place today. The boy on the left is Frederick Augustus Talbot Clifford-Constable (1828-94), wearing a tunic, worn by boys up to the age of ten. The carpet was probably fitted after building work in the 1830s, when the Long Gallery was extended. Cat. no. 9 and fig.12. (John Chichester Constable)

Plate 3. Detail of flat-woven carpeting, Kidderminster type, made in Barnard Castle, 1825-50, showing both sides of the reversible double cloth and the tape used to bind the edges. This simple diaper pattern was a very traditional design common in the eighteenth century. Before the Jacquard mechanism was employed, only such small-scale patterns could be produced on a draw-loom. Cat. no. 1.

Plate 4. Detail of flat-woven carpeting, Kidderminster type, British, late eighteenth or early nineteenth century, showing both sides of the reversible double cloth. The actual size of the motifs is similar to those shown in plate 3. The colours are also similar to the same three colours used for the warp threads. Cat. no. 2. (Colonial Williamsburg Foundation)

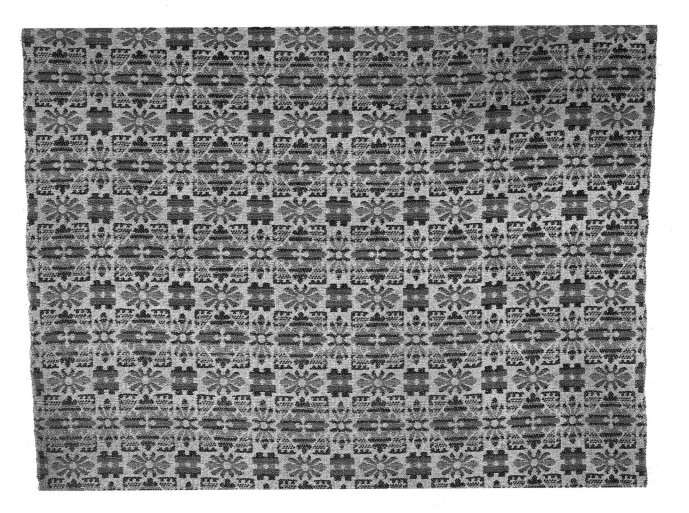

Plate 5. Strip of flat-woven carpet, showing a full width (33 inches), Kidderminster type, made in Barnard Castle about 1860, reversible double cloth (The reverse is shown in actual size on the back cover). The finding of a red synthetic dye has provided a date after 1860, when the first chemical dyes began to be used. By this date patterns had become larger and this geometric design would have been viewed as old-fashioned. Small-scale patterns probably enjoyed lasting popularity because there was less waste when joining widths. Cat.no. 3.

Plate 6. Detail of flat-woven carpeting, Kidderminster type, from Selkirk, Scotland, 1825-50, reversible double cloth. This type of carpeting, which Barnard Castle produced, was commonly called 'Scotch' carpet, as it had been made in Scotland from the middle of the eighteenth century. Cat. no. 5. (John Claridge, Selkirk)

CHAPTER 2

FASHIONS IN CARPETING

Until about 1780 carpets were regarded as a luxury. From the sixteenth century onward a steady stream of carpets from Turkey, Persia and India had been imported into Britain, such oriental carpets being considered the most luxurious of all. During the eighteenth century English carpet factories, such as Axminster and Moorfields, successfully produced their own hand-knotted carpets but these were also exclusive and expensive. By the end of the eighteenth century taste in interior design began to move away from grandeur and luxury towards informality and comfort and created fashions in decoration which could increasingly be imitated in middle-class interiors. Strip carpeting, hand woven in narrow widths and sold by the yard, was developed in the 1740's and gradually its advantages over oriental carpets began to be appreciated. Not only was it very much cheaper but it could be made to size with the colour and pattern chosen in advance. Such carpets were versatile, easy to cut and sew together to fit around hearths or into alcoves for wall-to-wall carpeting, or used in corridors or on stairs. And, in due course, they could be altered and used elsewhere. Brussels carpet, with a looped, uncut pile and Wilton carpeting, where the pile was cut, were the more expensive forms of strip carpeting and their use in country houses was widespread by the early-nineteenth century. A cheaper alternative was to use flat-woven carpeting, without a pile. This was not as hard-wearing but had the advantage of being reversible and could be turned when worn. The Long Gallery of Burton Constable Hall, near Hull, was fitted, wall-to-wall, with flat-woven carpeting in the 1830s, which can still be seen in place, today (plate 2 and fig. 12). More often in large houses, these cheaper carpets were the choice for small guest bedrooms, back corridors and staircases and the servants'

quarters; areas which required some comfort but should not demand too much in the way of expenditure.

The fashion for covering the floor with carpets steadily spread from the houses of the wealthy to a wider market. According to Whittock's *The Complete Book of Trades* in 1837 (p.113) 'The art of weaving carpets is carried on to a great extent in England at the present period, as they are now so generally used, not only by the more affluent classes of society, but by the middle and even the more humble classes; indeed there are few decent journeymen mechanics who have not a carpet of some kind to spread over their apartment on particular occasions; and it is scarcely possible to go into the parlour of a tradesman or shopkeeper without finding the floor carpeted'. The demand for affordable carpets had grown steadily from the early years of the century as the population increased and new homes were being built. This led to an expansion of the trade and the establishment of new centres, like Barnard Castle.

The main product of the Barnard Castle carpet looms was a flat-woven double cloth, called Kidderminster or 'Kidder', for short, after the town in Worcestershire where it was first reputedly made in 1735 (plates 3 & 5). By 1780, Kidderminster was established as the leading centre of carpet manufacture in England, but the production of the Kidderminster double cloth was even then being superseded by the more expensive Brussels carpeting woven with a durable, looped pile. This growing concentration on Brussels type by the weavers of Kidderminster left a gap in the market for the cheaper, flat-woven varieties - a gap which other towns were quick to exploit. Indeed, when their period of expansion came to an end in 1825, owing to a general slump in trade, Kidderminster manufacturers blamed the emergent competition in the North of England and Scotland. Their solution, to reduce the price paid to weavers from 1s to 10d a yard, was ineffective, as it resulted in a 5-month strike in 1828 and led some weavers to seek work elsewhere. 'The competition which had been feared became a reality, with other centres taking advantage of Kidderminster's cessation ..... their tenuous foothold [i.e. that of the other, newer centres] in the market was strengthened permanently' (Smith, 1984, 78).

The first of these centres in the North of England was in the County of Durham. Carpet weaving ventures had started up in the city of Durham, in Darlington and Barnard Castle as early as 1813, according to tradition, but by 1828 they were established and expanding. In a commentary by G. Layton to his poem *Castle Barnard* he states that 'Carpets are the principle article of manufactory; the chief part of the weavers are employed in this branch of the business. The colour of the carpets, from the superior water of the Tees, rivals those of Kidderminster in brilliancy and effect' (Layton, 1823). The number of carpet manufacturing firms in the West Riding of Yorkshire also grew impressively in this period, and on the other side of the Pennines, manufacturing of carpets began in Kendal in 1822, again developing from a thriving and long-established woollen industry.

In Scotland this same type of flat-woven carpeting had been made from the middle of the eighteenth century, hence its other common name 'Scotch' carpet (plate 6). In 1774, Edward Topham wrote of Scotland that carpets were 'their chief manufactory' and that 'the sale which these carpets meet with in England is astonishing; you find them in every house, from the highest to the lowest, as they are calculated to suit every class of people who wish the conveniences of life, but who cannot afford the extravagant prices of Wilton and Axminster, and other more expensive manufactories' (Topham, 1774-5, 175). Scotland's carpet

Fig. 8. *The Arrival of Country Relations* by Alexander Carse, about 1815. This accurate portrayal of a middle-class interior by a Scottish artist, shows a fitted carpet of geometric design, which almost certainly was a flat-woven Scotch type. Under the table is a crumb-cloth. (In the collection of the Duke of Buccleuch and Queensbury KT)

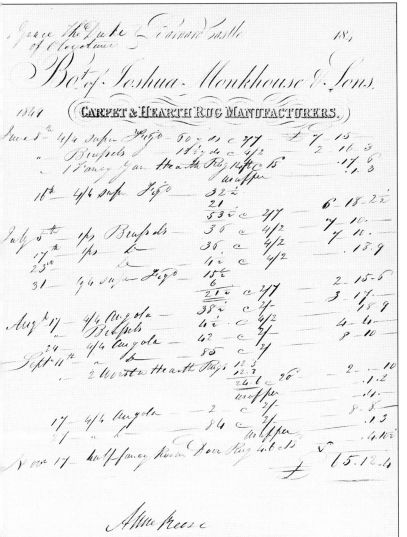

Fig. 9. Bill from Joshua Monkhouse & Sons, Barnard Castle to the Duke of Cleveland, Raby Castle, County Durham, 1849. It lists Brussels, 'Super Fig'd' [Venetian] and 'Angola' carpeting (see Chapter 3 and glossary), all ordered in 36in widths (4/4). In such large houses the use of these cheaper qualities would be confined to bedrooms and passages. Although *The Complete Book of Trades* (1837) may tell us that 'Journeyman mechanics' bought carpets, it is only the purchases by grander households which can usually be documented. (Lord Barnard)

industry continued to thrive, particularly in Kilmarnock throughout the nineteenth century (fig. 8). There was a continual movement of weavers between centres as trade thrived or failed and census figures show that there was some migration of weavers to Barnard Castle from other carpet-making centres (see Chapter 6).

Strip carpeting of the Kidderminster type was popular in the United States of America, where it was known as 'ingrain' because the yarn was dyed before weaving. America was Britain's main export market for carpets but the establishment of import tariffs in 1828 led to a decline in exports and encouraged American manufacturers, especially in Philadelphia (Kraak, 1996, 186).

The period 1840 to 1850 saw numerous technical improvements in carpet weaving, fuelled by the manufacturer's desire to meet the demand most profitably. In 1850, 60% of all the looms of the carpet industry in Great Britain were producing Kidderminster and other types of cheaper, flat-woven carpeting. At this date it was estimated that six of the sixteen largest carpet firms outside Kidderminster were in Barnard Castle. Monkhouse were fourth in the list, after Crossley of Halifax and two Scottish firms (Bartlett, 1978, 14).

Today, it is hard to realise just how extensively flat-woven carpets were used in homes as very little has survived. For those who could afford it, Brussels or Wilton was still the first choice for reception rooms, with flat-woven types used for bedrooms. However, Kidderminster had become widely accepted for use in drawing and sitting rooms of middle-class Victorian houses. In 1850 a 'sale by public competition' advertised in the *Darlington & Stockton Times*, 9 March, lists:

> Kidderminster carpet 6 1/2 yards long by 5 1/2 yards wide for Drawing Room .....
>
> 18 1/2 yards Dutch carpet in bedroom no 1 .....
>
> 15 yards Kidderminster carpet in bedroom no 2.

The contents of a large Victorian terrace house in Barnard Castle, going up for auction in 1894 reveals what was probably a fairly standard distribution of types of carpet:

> Kidder carpets in Back Sitting Room, Back Bedroom, Small Bedroom
>
> Tapestry Carpets in Front Bedroom
>
> Brussels carpets in Front Sitting Room, Stairs
>
> Hearthrugs in most rooms
>
> Mats in doorways

(*Teesdale Mercury*, 1 August 1894)

Kidderminster carpet, however, continued to be bought by all classes of society. Jacob Allison of Barnard Castle sold '72 1/2 yards of super kiddr. carpet' to J.B.S. Morritt of Rokeby Park in 1834 while in 1845 and 1849 Monkhouse was selling to the Duke of Cleveland for Raby Castle (fig. 9). The examples mentioned are of purchases for local houses, but a wider distribution was crucial for success. London was the premier market and it has been estimated that at least eighteen provincial manufacturers had warehouses and offices in London in 1840-1 (Barlett, 1978, 90). Both the firms of Pratt & Son and Monkhouse had London warehouse addresses. From the order books of Jacob Allison (see Chapter 7) it is clear that Barnard Castle carpets were distributed to the main wholesalers and retailers in London in the 1830s and thus reached the mass-market. According to Henderson 'Barnard Castle for several years exercised a very important influence upon the carpet trade in London and the Kingdom generally' (Henderson, 1863, 236).

However, after 1850, the introduction of power looms in the larger centres for the weaving of Brussels and Tapestry carpets resulted in greater and cheaper quantities being available. In the face of increasing competition, the Kidderminster types began to lose favour, particularly to the newly developed Tapestry carpeting, which could compete in price with the pile-less varieties. Brussels had always been dearer and cost 4s.1d per yard compared to 2s.6d per yard for Tapestry and Kidderminster in 1850 (Bartlett, 1978, 204). Mechanisation reduced the price of Brussels also, bringing it within the means of the majority of the carpet-buying public. Thus the less durable flat-woven carpets gradually lost favour. By the 1880s Kidderminster carpet was virtually eclipsed by an even cheaper quality of Tapestry carpet. The use of the power loom for weaving Kidderminster was adopted only slowly, due to lack of investment and the threat to the hand-loom weavers. However, some of the first broadloom carpets woven on power looms were of the Kidderminster type (Bartlett, 1978, 78). Inspired by a revival of fashion for oriental carpets, from about 1880 manufacturers successfully promoted seamless square Kidderminster carpets and called them 'Art Squares'. The ensuing demand was met by manufacturers mainly in the West Riding of Yorkshire and Scotland. Thus the fashion for carpets had come full circle, the difference being that seamless 'oriental style' carpets were no longer the exclusive prerogative of the rich. Barnard Castle appears to have entered this market just as the industry was declining, but could not compete with the mass production of the larger factories elsewhere.

CHAPTER 3

THE CARPETS OF BARNARD CASTLE

What did the actual carpets produced in Barnard Castle look like? Despite the thousands of yards that must have been woven there are few surviving specimens. Those which have survived are mainly the flat-woven Kidderminster type, also called Scotch, ingrain or two-ply carpeting. They were hand-woven, with woollen wefts and worsted warps. The maximum width of fabric was 36 inches, (referred to as 4/4), but narrower widths were also produced, expressed as fractions (i.e. 27 inches as 3/4, 22 inches as 5/8). Most were woven in a double cloth, which is composed of two fabrics which are woven simultaneously and interchange with each other. The pattern is formed by the woollen wefts which pass through to both sides at certain points in the pattern, thus joining the two fabrics. The same pattern is produced on both faces of the cloth, but the colours are reversed. The carpet shown in plate 3 (Cat. No.1) shows a detail of probably the earliest surviving example of this type of carpeting made in Barnard Castle. The small diaper pattern of this carpet has strong affinities with the simple lozenge designs of the late eighteenth century. It can be closely compared with a carpet in the Colonial Williamsburg Foundation, U.S.A. (plate 4, Cat. No. 2) which uses similar colours, in the same combination of shaded bands, in a pattern of the same scale. The Barnard Castle carpet is one of several identical pieces which are said to have been made from wool from Stoney Keld farm, Bowes, Teesdale, plucked from the sheep's back, spun in the farmhouse and woven at a Barnard Castle carpet factory especially for the family.

Fig. 10. Detail of 'Figured Venetian' carpeting from a small bedroom, Clifford's Tower, Raby Castle, probably supplied by Monkhouse & Sons, Barnard Castle, 1845-9. The small diaper design is in two shades of brown and cream. The warps alone form the visible surface of the carpet and the weft, which is a thick black woollen yarn, is completely hidden. Cat. no. 12 (Lord Barnard).

Another example of a traditional, formal pattern is shown in plate 5, Cat. No.3. This pleasing design of formalised rosettes and geometric motifs in a grid pattern suggests a date from the early years of the carpet weaving industry in Barnard Castle. However, this carpet contains a synthetic dye and must date from after 1860, proving that such patterns enjoyed lasting popularity. The pattern is a more sophisticated version of one used in a carpet reputed to date from the eighteenth century, woven at Troutbeck, Cumbria (Cat. No. 4) and can be seen in numerous Scottish examples, for example as shown in plate 6 (Cat. No.5).

Venetian carpet was a variant form of flat-woven carpeting. It was generally made in those centres which produced Kidderminster carpeting and Barnard Castle was no exception. It was woven on a simpler loom, as it was not double cloth and the pattern was made by the warp threads which totally concealed the wefts. Venetian carpeting was usually of a colourful, striped appearance, and commonly used as stair carpet or in corridors when woven in narrower widths. Although known to have been widely used in the nineteenth century, from frequent mention in bills and inventories, the only surviving carpeting which can so far be identified as Venetian was almost certainly made in Barnard Castle (Gilbert, 1987, 94). It dates from the 1860s and ran along a bedroom passage in Clifford's Tower, Raby Castle. (plate 7, Cat. No. 11).

In the Raby Castle archive is a bill from Joshua Monkhouse, Barnard Castle, dated 1845 which records earlier purchases of Venetian, with entries for '4/4 checked Venetian at 2/3d per yard, 4/4 super Figd. Venetian at 2/9d per yard, and 5/8 Venetian at 1/9d per yard'. In one of the bedrooms of Clifford's Tower, there is a fitted carpet which may be a 'super Figd. Venetian' as listed in the bill (fig. 10, Cat. No. 12).

251 MONKHOUSE, JOSHUA, & SON, *Barnard Castle*, and 75 *Wood Street, Cheapside, London*—Manufacturers.
Carpets, of Kidderminster fabric, cumber and point styles.
Dutch fabric carpets, all wool, and Dutch fabric carpets, warp made from silk noils.

252 MORTON & SONS, *Kidderminster*—Manufacturers.
Specimens of velvet pile carpets:—Crimson and colours (roses); ruby and chintz (flowers); crimson, green, &c. (lilies).
Saxony carpet:—crimson and oaks (scroll).
Brussels carpets:—white and gold (scroll); dark green and gold (ornament); royal blue and gold (ornament); ruby, crimson, and oaks (leaves); ruby, green, &c. (roses).

It has a small, diamond design, traditionally known as a 'bird's-eye' pattern. It was suggested in 1987, for the first time, that this type of pattern was likely to be that described in the nineteenth century as 'Figured Venetian' (Hefford, 1987, 5).

Another bill from Monkhouse to Raby Castle, dated 1849 (fig. 9), lists '4/4 Angola' at 2s.0d. a yard (the only known reference, so far, to such a type of carpeting) as well as 'Super Fig'd' Venetian, at 2s.7d. a yard and Brussels at 4s.2d. a yard. Angola yarn is a mixture of wool and cotton or other fibre. The name was applied to a fashionable fabric for shawls mixing wool with angora goat hair (mohair) in the early years of the nineteenth century (Montgomery, 1984, 147). Perhaps Angola was Monkhouse's own name for Dutch carpet with mohair noils, as opposed to the 'Dutch carpet with silk noils' they were exhibiting three years later at the Great Exhibition (fig. 11). Noils are the waste product after combing yarn and apparently the principal trade for mohair and alpaca noils 'was that of the Scotch, or Kidderminster carpet manufacture' (Beaumont, 1888, 17). The use of mohair noils would, like silk, add a certain brightness and sheen to the finished product. Dutch carpet was a cheaper product combining wool with other yarns in a single ply. A very recent discovery, covering a church kneeler, may be an example of the Dutch type (See Cat. No. 14). It is, however, impossible today to know precisely what was meant by names such as Dutch and Angola in the absence of documented specimens.

Fig. 11. Entry for Joshua Monkhouse and Son in *The Official Descriptive and Illustrated Catalogue of The Great Exhibition*, 1851, (Vol. II, Section III, 569). Of thirty entries for carpet manufacturers and producers only seven include Kidderminster. Henderson's of Durham call it 'ingrain', perhaps hoping to interest the American market. Like Morton & Sons, most of the manufacturers from Kidderminster displayed only Brussels, velvet pile and the new tapestry types. Crossley of Halifax were the only other exhibitor of Dutch carpeting. Monkhouses's entry uses the terms 'cumber' and 'point styles' (see glossary). No other firms used these descriptions. Specifying 'all wool' and 'silk noils' suggests a higher grade than ordinary Dutch.

Fig. 12. (Cat. no. 9) Piece of triple cloth carpeting from the Long Gallery, Burton Constable, near Hull. From a fitted carpet in brick red, light tan and cream, 1830-40, which is still in place, protected by a Brussels carpet overlayed in the 1860s. The effect of the large striking design can be seen in a coloured lithograph of the late 1830's, shown in plate 2. (John Chichester Constable).

The order book of Jacob Allison (Chapter 7) reveals the range and different qualities of carpeting he sold between 1823 and 1828. They included Super Kidder as well as Kidder, Dutch and Dutch Superfine. Other account books show that he was also producing Venetian and, from 1830, Damask carpeting. Damask appears to have been an improvement of the figured Venetian carpet. It was a combination of Kidderminster and Venetian, with a two-tone pattern.

There were a number of patents for improvements to the weaving process of these various types of flat-woven carpeting. The earliest patent, for double cloth in 1812, was to improve the size of the small repeating patterns. The patent by Thomas Pardoe, manufacturer of Kidderminster and

London, was for 'A new method of working or making carpeting denominated Kidderminster or Scotch' producing 'large, superior and more elegant designs than any that have been or can be produced' (Hefford, 1987, 4). A characteristic of Kidderminster carpet was its stripy appearance and this can clearly be seen in one of the Barnard Castle carpets (plate 8, Cat. No. 7). The large repeating medallion design appears to be superimposed over the top of the stripy ground formed by ingenious use of colours in the weft, forming bands across the widths. It is, in fact, a single colour design on a plain ground but the introduction of coloured stripes as a secondary, ground pattern, produces a richer effect. The effect was intentional: *The Penny Cyclopaedia* (1836, 313) tells us that Kidderminster 'may be woven in stripes of different shades' so 'the carpet is usually made to assume a great variety of colours'. A treatise on weaving (Watson, 1863, 288) explains that to 'have as many colours in the weft as there is in the warp makes a superior article. This may cause the use of a great number of shuttles, but it brings up fine, bright flowers where the same colour of weft and warp are made to cross each other'.

One of the most important developments in the weaving of pile-less carpeting was the invention of triple cloth or three-ply. This was the introduction of an additional layer between the two outer layers, creating a thicker, more robust carpet. Although patented by Thomas Lea of Kidderminster as early as 1812, there is no evidence that it eclipsed double cloth. By 1836 it was reckoned that double cloth formed 95% of production and that three-ply was for the North American market (*The Penny Cyclopaedia* 1836, 313). On a more encouraging note for the new invention, Ure's *Dictionary of Arts, Manufactures, and Mines* (1839; 7th ed, 1878, 733) states that 'The three-ply imperial carpet, called the Scotch, is coming very much into vogue, and is reckoned by many to be little inferior in texture, look and wear to the Brussels'. Henderson, writing in 1863, suggested that three-ply or Imperial Kidderminster was more a product of Scotland and valued at 2s 8d a yard, in 1850, rather than 2s 6d a yard for Kidderminster carpeting produced in England (Bartlett, 1978, 205). However, a piece of triple-weave carpet in The Bowes Museum with a local provenance (plate 9, Cat. No. 8) provides the best evidence that triple cloth was also produced in Barnard Castle. This single survivor is a bold imitation of a Turkish carpet design. Such Turkey patterns were very popular for carpets and painted floor cloths in the nineteenth century. Stronger, more sophisticated designs were possible in triple cloth even when limited to three colours and without the banding of colours associated with double cloth. As Wendy Hefford has pointed out, this is more in keeping with the large-scale curvilinear designs of nineteenth century carpeting. (Hefford, 1987, 5). Triple cloth was able to imitate the expansive designs first made fashionable in pile carpets. This can be seen to good effect in the triple cloth at Burton Constable Hall of about 1836-8, (fig. 12 and plate 2, Cat. No. 9), which is highly ambitious in its design.

By far the most important improvements for the making of strip carpeting were the major advances in weaving technology in the first half of the nineteenth century. Up to about 1825 carpets were hand-woven on a draw-loom. However the draw-loom did not lend itself easily to producing the patterns of double cloth. The handloom weaver, in order to create the pattern, required a drawboy to pull a cord for each heddle to lift the appropriate warp threads for the insertion of the weft for every line of the pattern. Patterned double-weaves, although woven in a balanced plain weave were nonetheless complicated to weave on a draw-loom and so the barrel-loom, invented in 1807, was an important development in the weaving of flat-woven carpets. The barrel was a patterning device studded with pins like a barrel organ, to select automatically the appropriate warps and lift them clear of the shuttle, thus reducing the risk of error by the drawboy who had previously done this task by hand. Thought to be invented by a Scot, John Duncan, the barrel, tambour or cylinder mechanism was described as the key element of his 'patent draw loom' (Sherrill, 1996, 218). Although an improvement, the barrel had to be changed for each new pattern, with a tedious alteration of the pins, and from about 1825 it began to be superseded by the Jacquard mechanism.

The Jacquard attachment further simplified the process, enabling intricate patterns to be woven with larger repeats. It, too, automatically selected and pulled the cords to control the warp threads without the need for a drawboy. However, the patterning mechanism employed punched cards which could be made and changed more easily and quickly than the barrel, thus increasing production (fig. 13). Generally the Jacquard was adopted by the carpet trade between 1825 and 1840. We do not know exactly when it was first introduced to Barnard Castle, but it was in use in Kidderminster in 1825 for the weaving of double cloth and patented in 1827 for the weaving of figured Venetian carpeting (Hefford, 1984, 5). Certainly by 1846 when Monkhouse built their new premises they had the high ceilings necessary for Jacquard towers or cylinders. These contained the punched cards which were laced together in a continuous chain high above the looms (fig. 14). The sale of John Pratt's looms and equipment in 1851 included a Jacquard machine, tools for cutting patterns and 'a large stock of cards and irons cut to Brussels, Kidderminster and Tapestry patterns' (fig. 15). The mention of irons might suggest the use of a barrel loom. In Scotland, these were still in use for Scotch carpet weaving in 1843 but were in the process of being replaced by the Jacquard (*The*

Fig. 13. Engraved illustration showing the making of punched cards for the Jacquard weaving mechanism from *The Pictorial Gallery of Arts* by Charles Knight (1858-60). Heavy cardboard cards were punched, based on a design first drawn on squared paper. The machine for stamping holes is on the left and the worker in the foreground is lacing cards together in a continuous chain. Once placed on the cylinder above the loom the holes in the card guided a needle and hook to raise the warps to produce the pattern.

Penny Magazine, 1843, 322). It is likely that Barnard Castle firms were also slow to change, particularly the smaller ones.

Barnard Castle was making Brussels carpeting from the 1820s, but there is no indication of the quantity produced. It was woven on special looms to produce a looped wool pile on a linen backing (fig. 16). The pile was formed by a worsted yarn of supplementary warps looped over wires

placed parallel to the weft, which were then withdrawn. According to Henderson the number of Brussels hand-looms fell from 17 to 2 between 1850 and 1863 in the County of Durham. The Brussels steam power loom had arrived in Durham City in 1854, but there is no evidence to suggest that it reached Barnard Castle. All that possibly remains of Barnard Castle's production of Brussels carpet are a number of fitted carpets in Raby Castle, possibly ordered from

Fig. 14. Scotch (or Kidderminster) carpet loom showing the Jacquard mechanism above, from *The Penny Magazine* August, 1843.

Joshua Monkhouse of Barnard Castle (plate 10 and fig. 9), and two small, unprovenanced fragments in The Bowes Museum.

By 1871, the *Teesdale Mercury* reported that manufacturing was flourishing again in the town and that '6 mills are wholly or partly driven by the Tees'. There is no indication whether these held power looms weaving Brussels or Kidderminster carpeting or an entirely different type of cloth. There is, however, one piece of evidence which suggests that Kidderminster broad-looms, probably steam powered, were introduced to Barnard Castle. A seamless double cloth carpet, almost eight feet wide, was given to The Bowes Museum in 1929, having been 'purchased in 1890 from Messrs. Dunns, Bridgegate Factory' as 'one of the last factory-made carpets in Barnard Castle' (fig. 17, Cat. No.13). In turning to the production of 'Art Squares', the manufacturers were making an effort to modernise until the moment of collapse of the industry.

Even when the trade was at its height, to be competitive, Barnard Castle manufacturers had to offer designs which the customer would find attractive. There was a growing demand for new patterns as the volume of production increased: '...the manufacturers compete with each other in the elegance of their patterns and excellence of their workmanship' (*The Complete Book of Trades,* 1837, 113). Every manufacturer wanted to be able to offer a large and varied selection and so, as in other branches of textile design, it was easier and cheaper to copy or adapt popular patterns than to invent new ones. Firms would produce a new range each year but some might be offered for several years, resulting in an enormous number of designs on the market. There were free-lance designers in the larger centres of carpet weaving, but even quite small carpet firms tended to employ their own designers, or pattern drawers. The manufacturers insisted that designers remained anonymous which was also the rule

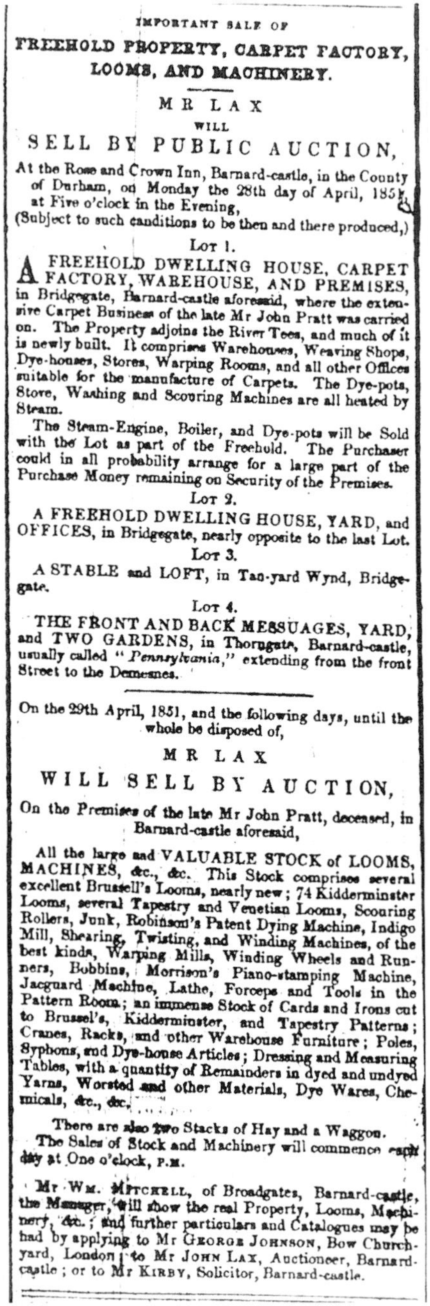

IMPORTANT SALE OF

FREEHOLD PROPERTY, CARPET FACTORY, LOOMS, AND MACHINERY.

MR LAX

WILL

SELL BY PUBLIC AUCTION,

At the Rose and Crown Inn, Barnard-castle, in the County of Durham, on Monday the 28th day of April, 1851, at Five o'clock in the Evening,

(Subject to such conditions to be then and there produced,)

LOT 1.

A FREEHOLD DWELLING HOUSE, CARPET FACTORY, WAREHOUSE, AND PREMISES, in Bridgegate, Barnard-castle aforesaid, where the extensive Carpet Business of the late Mr John Pratt was carried on. The Property adjoins the River Tees, and much of it is newly built. It comprises Warehouses, Weaving Shops, Dye-houses, Stores, Warping Rooms, and all other Offices suitable for the manufacture of Carpets. The Dye-pots, Store, Washing and Scouring Machines are all heated by Steam.

The Steam-Engine, Boiler, and Dye-pots will be Sold with the Lot as part of the Freehold. The Purchaser could in all probability arrange for a large part of the Purchase Money remaining on Security of the Premises.

LOT 2.

A FREEHOLD DWELLING HOUSE, YARD, and OFFICES, in Bridgegate, nearly opposite to the last Lot.

LOT 3.

A STABLE and LOFT, in Tan-yard Wynd, Bridgegate.

LOT 4.

THE FRONT AND BACK MESSUAGES, YARD, and TWO GARDENS, in Thorngate, Barnard-castle, usually called "*Pennsylvania,*" extending from the front Street to the Demesnes.

On the 29th April, 1851, and the following days, until the whole be disposed of,

MR LAX

WILL SELL BY AUCTION,

On the Premises of the late Mr John Pratt, deceased, in Barnard-castle aforesaid,

All the large and VALUABLE STOCK of LOOMS, MACHINES, &c., &c. This Stock comprises several excellent Brussell's Looms, nearly new; 74 Kidderminster Looms, several Tapestry and Venetian Looms, Scouring Rollers, Junk, Robinson's Patent Dying Machine, Indigo Mill, Shearing, Twisting, and Winding Machines, of the best kinds, Warping Mills, Winding Wheels and Runners, Bobbins, Morrison's Piano-stamping Machine, Jacguard Machine, Lathe, Forceps and Tools in the Pattern Room; an immense Stock of Cards and Irons cut to Brussel's, Kidderminster, and Tapestry Patterns; Cranes, Racks, and other Warehouse Furniture; Poles, Syphons, and Dye-house Articles; Dressing and Measuring Tables, with a quantity of Remainders in dyed and undyed Yarns, Worsted and other Materials, Dye Wares, Chemicals, &c., &c.

There are also two Stacks of Hay and a Waggon.

The Sales of Stock and Machinery will commence each day at One o'clock, P.M.

MR WM. MITCHELL, of Broadgates, Barnard-castle, the Manager, will show the real Property, Looms, Machinery, &c.; and further particulars and Catalogues may be had by applying to MR GEORGE JOHNSON, Bow Churchyard, London; to MR JOHN LAX, Auctioneer, Barnard-castle; or to MR KIRBY, Solicitor, Barnard-castle.

Fig. 15. Advertisement for the auction sale of Pratt's Carpet Factory, *Darlington & Stockton Times*, 12 April 1851. Evidence for the scale of manufacture and the types of carpeting produced by one of the larger Barnard Castle firms. Kidderminster was mainly woven (74 looms) but also Brussels, Venetian and Tapestry. The last was unlikely to be for the recently invented printed pile variety which required large printing rollers, but probably a version of the simplest flat-woven carpet. The detailed list of machinery reveals all the necessary processes: scouring, dyeing, warping, Jacquard card making (presumably on Morrison's piano stamping machine) (Darlington Public Library).

at the International Exhibitions. No evidence has come to light about carpet designers in Barnard Castle, either working for particular firms or self-employed. Jacob Allison's order books show a great number of different designs on offer, denoted by numbers, but the accounts reveal that he only once paid for sketches. Between 1824 and 1829 Allison sold twenty-six different designs, nearly all Kidderminster, and each year up to five new designs appeared (see Chapter 7). Designs might also be provided by the customers, who retained the patent rights to such designs. A firm such as Riley and Lapworth, 20 Old Bond Street, London (a regular customer of Allisons in Barnard Castle in the 1830s) described themselves as 'Carpet Manufacturer' even though they owned no mills. They sub-contracted the weaving,

Fig. 17. Detail of a Kidderminster broad-loom carpet, showing a corner of the border and centre-field design in reds, brown and buff, Barnard Castle, 1890. Cat. No. 13.

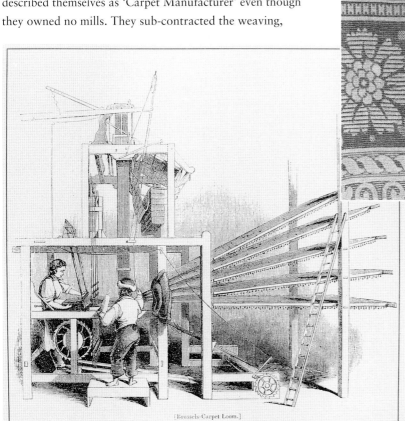

[Brussels-Carpet Loom.]

Fig. 16. Brussels carpet loom with Jacquard mechanism from *The Penny Magazine*, August 1843. The looped pile is formed over rods, which are inserted and withdrawn as the weaving progresses; hence the need for the weaver's assistant.

probably commissioning to their own exclusive designs (Bartlett 1978, 78).

Three of the Barnard Castle carpet firms took advantage of new laws to register designs, to protect them from plagiarism. This suggests that they had their own designers and wanted to ensure that their patterns remained exclusive. A total of seventeen designs for carpets from the three firms of Pratt, Son & Co., Richard Dunn and Monkhouse, Whitfield & Co, registered between 1842 and 1853, have been found in the Design Registers kept at the Public Record Office (Kew). In 1842 a Design Act was passed which gave three year's protection to ornamental designs. Carpet manufacturers could send a point paper (design on graph paper), tracing, watercolour, or a woven sample to obtain copyright. The designs from Barnard Castle are in the form of point papers and provide a valuable insight into the range of designs available from these firms. Although nothing is known about the majority of the designs, this small sample can be assumed to be fairly representative. The firm of John and Francis Kipling of Darlington (sixteen miles from Barnard Castle) registered thirty-two designs over the same

Fig. 19. Point paper no. 2541, Pratt, Son & Co, Barnard Castle, 1 December, 1842 (17 x 14 cm).

Fig. 20. Point paper no. 2542, Pratt, Son & Co, Barnard Castle, 1 December, 1842 (18 cms x 13 cm). The inscription 'No. 1005' may, in this case, refer to the firm's design number. This design has been reproduced by Hugh Mackay Carpets, Durham for The Bowes Museum's staircase in 1996.

Fig. 18. Point paper no. 2540, Pratt, Son & Co., Barnard Castle, 1 December, 1842 (8 x 18 cm).

period which are very similar to those produced by the Barnard Castle firms. The seventeen designs from Barnard Castle are graphed on to squared paper (sixteen squares to the inch) and all, except two, have the design painted in red ink onto the white ground of the paper. These are point papers from which the design could be woven in double or triple cloth or in a Brussels looped pile. They could be very simply interpreted into three- or four-colour designs as in plate 11 (Cat. no. 6) or elaborated by the introduction of bands of colours across the weft as seen in plate 8 (Cat. no. 7). Most of the point papers are from Pratt, Son & Co, of Bridgegate, who registered six in 1842, seven in 1844, and one in 1845 (B.T.43. 105-108). The earliest group, from 1842, uses bold formal motifs, two designs per sheet, suggesting a border and main body pattern. Design no. 2540 (fig.18) has a border of interlinked ovals, the body a geometric design of elongated crosses within quatrefoils. Such classically-inspired geometric panels are sometimes combined with flowing naturalistic forms. For example, no. 2541, (fig. 19), brings together a Greek key border with a large scale seaweed design and no. 2542 (fig. 20), a border of linked rectangles, combined with a strapwork and arabesque design.

The patterns of 1844 are of a more flowing, floral nature, but like those above are standard stock-in-trade designs of the period. A typical example (no. 18146, fig.21) has tightly scrolling acanthus

bordering a loose, spriggy design with flowers and hart's tongue fern. Similar floral patterns, with fern-like leaves, are to be found on printed cottons of the decade. The Rococo Revival of the 1830's can be seen in the ribbon-like trails and naturalistic flowers in no. 16170, (fig. 22). This mix of different historical styles is typical of the second quarter of the nineteenth century. There was a proliferation of books of ornament throughout this period, disseminating a wide range of styles to choose from.

Fig. 22. Point paper no. 16170, Pratt, Son & Co., Barnard Castle, 13 February, 1844 (43 x 75 cm).

Fig. 21. Point paper no. 18146, Pratt, Son & Co., Barnard Castle 2 May, 1844 (13 x 18 cm).

Towards the middle of the nineteenth century, the prevailing taste for revivals led to a confusion of styles, perfectly illustrated by the over-elaborate design registered by Monkhouse, Whitfield & Co., (no. 27503, (B.T. 43.108)) in 1845. This ambitious polychrome Chinoiserie design, including Greek fret, minarets and flowers, was perhaps registered with an exhibition in mind (plate 12). It was a brave attempt to put the products of Barnard Castle on an international platform but was the epitome of what design reformers of the period were opposing: the argument went that carpets were meant to be trodden on and were more suited to two-dimensional designs than illusionistic effects (Sherrill 1996, 291-3).

However, this design seems to have been a single wild flight of fancy for the Barnard Castle manufacturers. A design by Pratt's of the same year (no. 29753) has none of that extravagance and successfully combines a tesselated, mosaic pavement design, typically seen in painted floor cloths, with flowers and tendrils (fig. 23). The last designs from Barnard Castle to be registered were by Richard Dunn in 1851 and 1853 (B.T. 43.114 & 115). The first is a bold leaf and sea-weed design employing three colours with a dark ground, no. 80130 (plate 13). His design of 1853 (no. 91996) is more reminiscent of oriental patterns, perhaps influenced by the admiration of the contemporary design reformers for Eastern carpet design. In Barnard Castle it was clear that carpet designers were following the fashions. They relied on traditional and well-established motifs: the variations of use of motifs in the registered designs suggest proprietors and designers playing safe. They were providing for essentially conservative markets which were unlikely to take risks in buying an item of furnishing which (though inexpensive in relation to piled carpet) represented a heavy investment of household income. Sadly, this cautious attitude was not to serve the manufacturers well: one of the reasons given by Henderson (1863, 236) for the decline of Barnard Castle carpet trade was that the manufacturers were content to follow in the footsteps of other firms, seldom originating new patterns.

Fig. 23. Point paper no. 29753, Pratt, Son & Co., Barnard Castle, 14 August, 1845 (22 x 22 cm).

Plate 7. Strip of Venetian carpet, showing the full width, 22 inches, probably made in Barnard Castle about 1860, from Raby Castle, County Durham. This complex and colourful striped Venetian is the only known example of a type of carpeting that was once common in the nineteenth century. It was mainly used in corridors and on stairs. Cat. no. 11 (Lord Barnard)

Plate 8. Detail from a flat-woven carpet showing half of one of the three strips it is made up of, and a hand-sewn seam joining the widths. Kidderminster type, made in Barnard Castle, 1840-60, reversible double cloth. This large design, two medallions across the 36 inch width, would have probably been woven on a loom with a Jacquard mechanism. It illustrates the 'stripy' effect which was so characteristic of Kidderminster carpeting; the design is seen against bands of changing colours in the weft. Cat. no. 7.

Plate 9. A strip of flat-woven carpeting showing a full width of 33 inches, Kidderminster type, made in Barnard Castle about 1850, reversible triple cloth. This is the only known example of triple cloth from Barnard Castle and is woven in an imitation of Turkish carpet design. Cat. no. 8.

Plate 10. Brussels carpeting in a small bedroom, Raby Castle, probably made in Barnard Castle by Joshua Monkhouse & Son, 1845-9. One of a number of small bedrooms still carpeted with this type of carpet, which has a looped pile. Monkhouse's bills to Raby indicate that large quantities of Brussels were supplied in 1845 and 1849. Other firms in the town also made Brussels, but their chief products were the various types and qualities of flat-woven carpet. Inset shows a close-up of the lattice body pattern and the rosette design of the separate border. A Brussels border of the same design has been found in the Moot Hall, Newcastle upon Tyne, used as a narrow stair runner but with a different body pattern. It has been reproduced by Hugh Mackay Carpets, Durham. (Lord Barnard)

CHAPTER 4

Carpet Manufacturers in Barnard Castle

The title of Carpet Manufacturer was adopted by those who managed the making of carpets; manufacturers were not necessarily textile workers of any kind, but they were, rather, the people who provided the capital, formed the marketing contacts, arranged for new buildings and machinery, supervised the workforce and carried out the day-to-day management of the companies.

A company could employ scores, or even hundreds of people. Its size was judged by either number of looms or number of workers. Usually one loom could keep two workers employed.

In Barnard Castle there were many people who called themselves manufacturers. Little record exists in directories or other printed sources of the manufacturers Crampton & Willis; Thomas Ellary; Winskill, Jordan & Hildreth; James Alderson; Winpenny & Middleton; or the Peacock family. Very much more is known about those companies in the town, which are listed in William Henderson's British Association paper of 1863. These had owned, in 1836, a total of 428 looms. Henderson's estimate, made when the carpet trade was well established, shows the following companies:

Messrs. Monkhouse	130 looms
Mr. Pratt	80 looms
Messrs. Atkin & Co.	60 looms
Messrs. Dunn & Ramshaw	54 looms
Mr. John Winskill	38 looms
Mr. Raine	36 looms
Mr. J. Winskill	30 looms

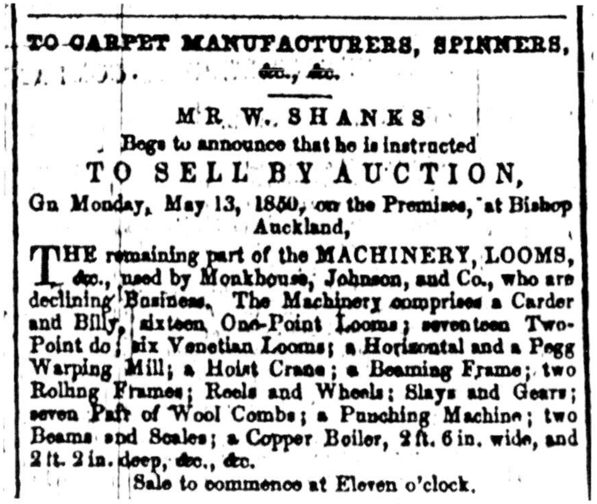

TO CARPET MANUFACTURERS, SPINNERS, &c., &c.

MR. W. SHANKS

Begs to announce that he is instructed

TO SELL BY AUCTION,

On Monday, May 13, 1850, on the Premises, at Bishop Auckland,

THE remaining part of the MACHINERY, LOOMS, &c., used by Monkhouse, Johnson, and Co., who are declining Business. The Machinery comprises a Carder and Billy, sixteen One-Point Looms; seventeen Two-Point do; six Venetian Looms; a Horizontal and a Pegg Warping Mill; a Hoist Crane; a Beaming Frame; two Rolling Frames; Reels and Wheels; Slays and Gears; seven Pair of Wool Combs; a Punching Machine; two Beams and Scales; a Copper Boiler, 2 ft. 6 in. wide, and 2 ft. 2 in. deep, &c., &c.

Sale to commence at Eleven o'clock.

Fig. 24. Auction notice, 1850, of residual equipment from the factory run by Ebenezer Monkhouse and a partner in Bishop Auckland from about 1835, *Darlington & Stockton Times,* 11 May 1850. The items offered were probably obsolescent, since the carpet industry generally was moving away from flat-woven carpets, towards Brussels and Tapestry types, and many aspects of production were becoming mechanised. The range of equipment suggests a factory with wool-preparation and spinning, as well as weaving, and the presence of a Punching Machine suggests the use of Jacquard looms. (Darlington Public Library)

Several indications exist of company sizes around the mid century: according to an obituary article about Joshua Coke Monkhouse (1815-90), his family firm had employed 150 hands in 1845. (*Teesdale Mercury,* 3 December 1890). In 1849, John Pratt was said, also in an obituary notice, to employ 200 to 300 people. (*Darlington & Stockton Times,* 6 September 1849). In 1850, Ebenezer Monkhouse at his Bishop Auckland factory (he had set up independently of the Barnard Castle firm) had for sale thirty-nine looms for flat-weave carpet including six Venetian looms (*Darlington & Stockton Times,* 11 May 1850, - fig. 24). The following year, Pratts's offered for sale 74 Kidderminster looms, and several of other types (*Darlington & Stockton Times,* 12 April 1851, - fig. 15). The 1851 census shows Edward Raine employed twenty-four men, nineteen boys and four females. In 1874, according to J.N. Bartlett, Joseph Hepworth, a partner of the late Richard Dunn, had twelve looms and twenty-four workers (Bartlett, 1978, 210).

A study of the accounts of Jacob Allison suggests that one weaver could make one piece of yard-wide carpet some eighty-eight to ninety yards long in about a week. Barnard Castle was therefore the scene of only a moderate-sized industry, though one of considerable importance to a small town.

The manufacturers in Barnard Castle adopted business methods similar to those noted in contemporary Kidderminster by Dr. L.D. Smith (Smith, 1982). He identifies three business formations: a family firm in which relatives provided all the skills; a partnership in which various skills in business or in textiles were brought together by the members; and a sole proprietorship.

A good example of a family firm in Barnard Castle was the company of Pratt & Son. 'Pratt' was Thomas Pratt (1775-1846) and 'Son' was John Pratt (1802-49). The family had been occupied in the weaving trade for several generations. There is no indication of any partners outside the family. There is however some evidence of family prosperity. Thomas's sister Ann, who died in 1832, referred in her will to real-estate, money on loan, clothing and jewellry. Thomas left a personal estate worth £450, and John left an estate worth just under £8,000, including the carpet company. The company was able not only to manufacture, but also to design its products; the designs now extant are discussed in Chapter 3. The buildings were offered for sale in 1851 as Pratts' own property, and were said to be, in part, newly built (fig.15).

A company which used the partnership system quite extensively was Dunn's. The principal in this firm, Richard Dunn

(1787-1871) invested considerable money of his own - his will shows that he had £4,000 placed in the business. But Dunn was not a textile expert, and so formed partnerships with men of more relevant experience. Early partners were Harrison and Crosby. Harrison's identity is still uncertain, but Parker Crosby (born about 1775 at Sedbergham, near Carlisle), was a cotton-manufacturer, who had married a daughter of the local Ewbank family. After his wife died in 1828, he turned to keeping The Angel Inn - there were young children - and was well-known in the town. Another partner was John Ramshaw, but this partnership ended in 1841, when Ramshaw died suddenly at Barningham. Initially, Dunn and Ramshaw were manufacturers of Plaid and Stuff, listed as such in Pigot's *Directory* of 1828, and so were well-placed to take up carpet making when the market arose. Richard Dunn was so unfortunate as to have lost a number of close relatives early in life. His brother Frank died in 1840, and Frank's eldest son Richard in 1851. Richard Dunn the manufacturer had no children, so that the future of the company presented a problem. This he resolved in 1858, by forming a partnership with an experienced carpet-maker Joseph Hepworth (1810-91), to whom in his will he left the management of the company until his great-nephew, also called Richard, reached the age of twenty-five.

The Monkhouse company started as a partnership, but became a family firm. The earliest Monkhouse to be concerned with carpets was Joshua Monkhouse (1792-1866). A son of a gingerbread baker, he was a grocer in the Market Place. This background would suggest that his contribution to carpet-manufacture might be financial, or that he might bring knowledge of marketing or of purchasing. Joshua's youngest brother, Ebenezer Monkhouse (1798-1863) was probably included in the carpet venture. An early partner was a Mr. Dixon, who seems likely to be William Dixon

(1769-1829) or possibly his brother Thomas Dixon (1751-1826), sons of a prominent local textile-manufacturing family. Thomas Dixon's imposing tombstone in the church-yard at Barnard Castle is inscribed "The BURIAL PLACE of the family of Thomas Dixon, Manufacturer". Entries in parish registers show that Thomas began as a weaver before being named as a manufacturer, and once as a manufacturer of serges. William was a linen weaver, and later a linen drap-er. Another early partner was Mr. Whitfield, who can be identified as Mr. John Whitfield, (born 1771), son of a wealthy family from Startforth, across the river from Barnard Castle. Wills held by The Borthwick Institute, University of York, show that John Whitfield inherited from his father, John Whitfield the Elder (died March 1824), real-estate includ-ing a house at Church Style, Barnard Castle, and considerable wealth. He inherited also a major part of the estate of his uncle William Whitfield (1753-1824). The first of these estates was worth up to £7,000 and the sec-ond up to £2,000, so that although John's brothers and sisters also benefited, he must nevertheless have become quite well-to-do. Both John and his half-brother, George (born 1784) were cheesemongers and lived in London in the Regent Street area, John in Lamb's Conduit Street, and George in Foubert's Place. Years afterwards, people recollected in a *Teesdale Mercury* article that there had been a partner who resided in London (*Teesdale Mercury*, 3 December 1890). In the 1840s the sons of Joshua Monkhouse: Joshua Coke Monkhouse (1815-90), Jeremiah Robert Monkhouse(born 1816) and John Wesley Septimus Monkhouse (born 1828) joined the business. The title of the firm changed to reflect the varying management: In 1822, according to the Barnard Castle Watch Book, quot-

ed in the *Teesdale Mercury* 25 December 1895, it was Monkhouse and Dixon; in 1829 Pigot's *Directory* named it as Monkhouse, Dixon and Whitfield; then Monkhouse and Whitfield, so described in the *Teesdale Mercury* obituary notice for J.C. Monkhouse (3 December 1890); then Joshua Monkhouse & Sons - the initials JM & S^s appear on the 1846 factory wall: and last of all, in Slater's *Directory* for 1854, after the retirement of Joshua Monkhouse himself, it became Monkhouse Brothers (fig. 25).

Sole proprietorships were not usual in Barnard Castle, and seemed to arise for relatively short periods when a partner-

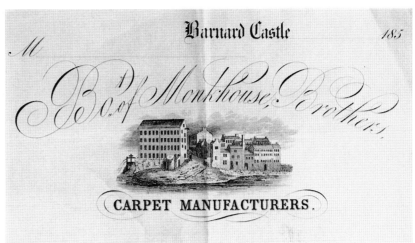

Fig. 25. Bill-head from the leading Barnard Castle manufacturer 1850-9. The view is taken from the south bank of the River Tees based on R. Harley's drawing (fig. 5). The factories are situated east and west of Thorngate. To the left of the picture is Thorngate Mill, (still standing), built 1847-8, on the site of a former sawmill, and using the existing weir and race, with its outlet sluice visible to the left (west) of the building. East of Thorngate, the gable end of the 1846 factory (now converted to houses) is clearly visible. It was on the site to the right of the picture that Monkhouse's first manufactory was established about 1820, close to the river. The buildings shown in this picture probably include that early industrial development, but the area was substantially redeveloped in the later nineteenth century. The Monkhouse partnership did its own dyeing, and this activity may account for the doors giving access to the water, and for the industrial chimney on the river bank (North of England Open-Air Museum, Beamish).

ship had ended. Jacob Allison and Edward Raine both seem to have worked independently at some periods of their working lives.

If a takeover, a bankruptcy or a merger took place, the existing manufacturer might be offered employment in the new company. This was more likely to happen if the man had specific skills in textiles than if he were a businessman - Edward Raine, for example, was employed for many years as manager of the very business in which he had failed on his own account . Raine's obituary in the *Teesdale Mercury* (30 January 1867) presents a sympathetic view of his business difficulties, and a very favourable view of other attributes.

The men who began these carpet companies were educated, middle-class people. They often belonged to Non-conformist religious groups; the Monkhouse family and the Dixon family were dedicated Methodists, whose relatives included local preachers and ministers and who named their children after notable Methodists such as Joshua Coke and John Wesley. Edward Raine from his nineteenth year was a member of the Presbyterian (now the United Reformed) Church. Jacob Allison was a Quaker, a member of the Cotherstone Meeting. A principal reason for this cultural setting was that entry to the universities and therefore to the major professions, was limited to Church of England members, so that men of other persuasions must try to make their fortunes in industry instead. Textile workers themselves did not need to be literate to produce their goods, but they needed the skills offered by these entrepreneurs if they were to develop their business beyond a local level.

Most companies seem to have relied heavily on the London trade, and either dealt regularly with a specific range of wholesalers, as Jacob Allison did, or appointed a London warehouseman. The warehouseman for Pratt's about 1849

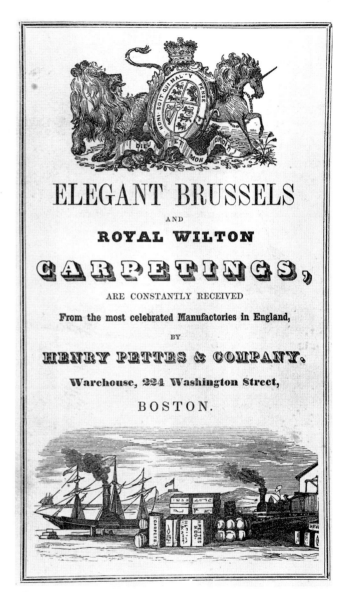

Fig. 26. Cover of a catalogue of Pettes & Co., Boston, U.S.A. probably 1840s, indicating the huge trade in carpet exports from Britain. The advertiser shows that the most modern steam trains and ships were used to transport the carpets in the United States. Barnard Castle's failure to achieve a railway link was a major cause of the decline of the carpet industry in the town (The Winterthur Library, Printed Book and Periodical Collection).

was George Johnson of Bow Churchyard, who became John Pratt's executor, and Monkhouse's was R. Margetson of 75 Wood Street, which was in the City. Members of the family or of the partnership might live in London, or go there very frequently - it seemed to be the practice to send a young son, or a younger brother. When Monkhouse's new buildings were inaugurated in 1848, the youngest son Mr. J.W.S. Monkhouse was away in London and could not participate in the festivities (*Darlington & Stockton Times*, 26 February 1848). A manufacturer might also sell direct to a retailer in a large city; and sales were also made locally, even to individual householders. The account (Chapter 7) of Jacob Allison's trading methods shows how such arrangements operated.

It is not known to what extent carpets from Barnard Castle were exported, but it is possible that some of the products were. Export could have been carried out by the London warehouses, so that records of it would not appear in the books of local firms. Certainly in the first half of the nineteenth century export to America was an important part of the British carpet trade. A handbill from a catalogue of Henry Pettes & Co.., Boston, Mass. shows a scene on a quayside, with ships and a railway in evidence, with crates and rolls of carpets awaiting carriage. Similar scenes could have been observed wherever the goods were sent (fig. 26).

For Allison and probably for the other manufacturers, transport to London was by road to Stockton and then by coastal steamer. Carriers in Barnard Castle were used, such as the Harrison family (fig. 27), and must have received a good deal of business.

From Stockton, shipping companies developed an efficient service to London. An early company was The Maritime Company, founded in 1803 to provide shipping services to ports at home and abroad. In 1806, The Merchants'

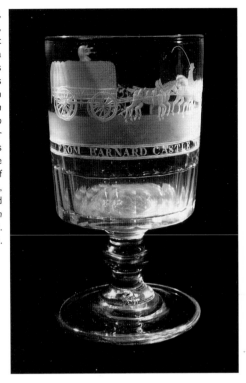

Fig. 27. Goblet, glass, about 1820, the upper part engraved with a scene of six horses pulling a carrier's cart. Underneath, an inscription *From Barnard Castle to Stockton*. The other side of the bowl is engraved with the arms of Harrison of Stubb House, Barnard Castle and the name *William Harrison* underneath. Height: 18.9 cm.

Shipping Company was formed with a concentration on the London trade. This company had a fleet of eight vessels in the range 105 to 120 tons, with sailings timetabled to allow one sailing at the end of every week from each of the ports of London and Stockton. The United Shipping Company was then re-formed as The Stockton Shipping Company to create competition. A contemporary author, John Brewster, gives a precise account of the setting-up of these companies, which were felt to bring great prestige to the town of Stockton (Brewster, 1829, 217-8). Manufacturers might have shares in a shipping company. In 1819, the Barnard Castle woollen manufacturer, Henry Ewbank, left to his daughter, Hannah, £600 and his shares in the Merchants' Shipping Company (D.C.R.O.).

The names of several of the vessels are known - the 'Tees' and the 'Thames', the 'Wynyard', the 'Cleveland' and the 'Raby Castle', the 'Majestic' and the 'Alert', the 'Fanny', the 'Emerald Isle' and the 'James Watt'. A sailing bill shows that in 1828, the 'Cleveland' was owned by the Merchants' company, and Richard Hill was her Master (fig. 28). She sailed for Stockton from Hay's Wharf (in Southwark) on Saturdays, and the last day for taking goods on board was Friday. At Stockton, she would berth at J. Wilkinson's Wharf. The return journey from Stockton would be begun on a Thursday, 'wind and weather permitting'. She carried passengers as well as goods, and enabled more than one hundred towns and villages in an area bordered by Ripon, Kendal, Keswick, Durham City and the seacoast to be reached by road from the seaport (Ellis, 1952, 48).

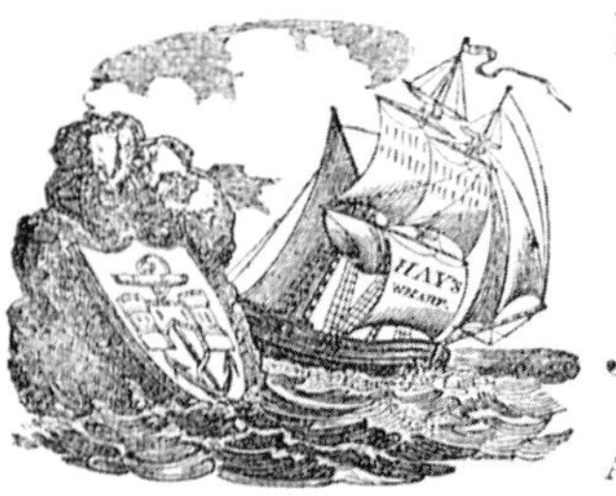

New Merchants' Shipping Company's
VESSELS
SAIL EVERY SATURDAY
FROM HAY'S WHARF,
LONDON,
TO
J. WILKINSON & Co.'s WHARF,
STOCKTON,
And from thence to London, every Thursday:—Wind and Weather permitting.

AT HAY'S WHARF, SOUTHWARK, IS NOW LOADING,

For STOCKTON,

The CLEVELAND, Richard Hill, Master,

To Clear on Saturday

Takes in Goods and Passengers for the following Places:—

APPLEBY	Carlton	Egglescliffe	KENDAL	Ormesby	Swainby
Ambleside	Coxhow	Fishburn	Kilvington	Osmotherly	Sheraton
Ackliff	Cornforth	Gunnerside	Kirby-stephen	Pickhill, Potto	Southchurch
Askrig	Comondale	Gilling, Gayles	Kirkleatham	Piersbridge	Summerhouse
Ayton, Ask	Crakehall	GUISBOROUGH	KESWICK	PENRITH	Trimdon
Aldborough	Cross Lane	Gainsford	LEYBURN	Ravenstonedale	Templesowerby
Barton	Castle Eden	HELMSLY	Lofthouse	Raby	Topcliffe
Brancepeth	Carthorp	Hart	Marsk	Reet	THIRSK
Billingham	Catheric	Hurworth	MASHAM	RICHMOND	Tanfield
Brompton	Castleton	Haughton	MIDDLEHAM	Redcar, RIPON	Upleatham
Brotton	Crathorne	Hartlepool	Middleton Tyas	Sedgefield	Welbury
Barnard Castle	Churchborough	Hawes	Middleton-in-Teesdale	Skelton	Wynyard
BEDALE	Cockfield	Hunton		STAINDROP	Wolviston
Bishopton	Downholm	Harlsey	Morland	STOCKTON	West Layton
Bishop Auckland	DARLINGTON	Hutton Rudby	Newby-wisk	STOCKSLEY	East Layton
Brough, Bowes	Danby-wisk	Kirkoswald	Northallerton	Staithes	Worsal
Borrowby	DURHAM	Kingsmeaburn	Norton	Shap	West Auckland
Cleasby	Eaglestone	Kirbymoorside	Normanby	Sedburgh	YARM

And all Places adjacent in Yorkshire, Durham, Westmoreland, Cumberland, &c., contiguous to the River Tees.—The Master or Wharfinger to be spoke with at the said Wharf, or on the Irish Walk in 'Change hours.

Not to advise of Goods being shipped till they are on board. W. HUMPHERY, Wharfinger.

THE LAST DAY OF TAKING IN GOODS IS FRIDAY.

Not accountable for loss by fire or leakage, the act of God, the King's enemies, and all and every other damage or accident to which Goods are subject on the sea, rivers, and navigation, of what nature or kind soever, to which the Master or Crew on board the Ship have in no way been accessary.

Please to send the Particulars of what the Packages contain, and Money for Wharf charges.

1828. Wharfage and Sufferance, £ s. d.

C. Raine

Eliz. Soulby, Printer and Stationer, 91, Gracechurch-Street.

Fig. 28. Shipping Bill, Hay's Wharf, 1829. On 24 March 1835 Jacob Allison of Barnard Castle sent four pieces of carpet to Hay's Wharf, Tooley Street, Southwark, by this ship, 'The Cleveland'. The bill shows how wide a range of townships were served by road from the Port of Stockton (Hays plc).

CHAPTER 5

INDUSTRIAL PREMISES

In Barnard Castle industrial premises were at first established within the curtilages of the owners' houses. The Town Plan dated 1827 (fig. 1) shows how houses south of Bridgegate had long plots of land to the rear, sometimes reaching the riverbank. These houses were most desirable to manufacturers in the tanning, brewing and woollen industries. The weaver Ferdinando Ewbank (died 1759) occupied as tenant 'all that messuage ... dyehouse and tenement with the work-house, brewhouse, dyehouse, stable and backbuildings, garth, garden and yard ... on the south side of Bridgegate' (Hanby-Holmes 3/2/22(1)). Here was accommodation suitable for a variety of trades. Ewbank was able to acquire the property, which he then bequeathed to his sons William and Joseph, together with the pump and various vessels in the dyehouse, for 'sizing ... and other uses' (Hanby-Holmes 3/2/26). In 1835, an abstract of title to property formerly belonging to Joseph Ewbank and his son Henry referred to a freehold house and carpet manufactory in Thorngate, with 'Dyehouse, Pumps, Cisterns, Boilers, Leads and Utensils' (Hanby-Holmes 2/7/449). These were the premises used by Jacob Allison in the period 1827 to 1835 (Chapter 7). Typical dwelling-houses dating from the eigh-

Fig. 29. Bridgegate, Barnard Castle, the south side during demolition in the mid-twentieth century. The house to the left of the picture, the home of Edward Raine, still stands. In the eighteenth century, these houses were occupied by weavers, dyers, tanners and brewers, whose work-shops were situated in the long back-gardens leading down to the River Tees. The dignity of the frontages suggests prosperous owners.

teenth century are shown in photographs taken when Bridgegate was demolished in the mid twentieth century (fig. 29). The arrangement of house with industrial premises is exemplified by the present 1996 Bridgegate Tyres Depot. A recent drawing (fig. 30) shows the house much as it could have looked when it was first built in the eighteenth century, except that the arch to the left of the front door was originally intended for vehicular traffic entering the yard, and would have had wooden doors.

The mill building, to the rear of this dwellinghouse, has a loading-door, (plate 14) which certainly gave good access to the water and could even allow for shallow-draft boats; the level of the river would have been higher in those days, because of the nearby 'warren' or weir and although the Tees was not a navigable river at this point, yarns, dyes etc. were almost certainly moved short distances by boat. The mill itself was purpose-built in 1839 (figs 31-2) for carpet looms, of which the owner, Mr. Raine, was said to have thirty-six in 1836 (Henderson, 1863, 236). The appearance inside suggests that looms could have been ranged along each wall, near to the windows, with a gangway in the centre. A 1996 photograph shows the building in use as a tyre depot, and the presence of the tyres usefully indicates the scale of the interior (fig. 33). This building might have held up to 30 looms on each floor but space would be needed also for warping-frames or other ancillary equipment. It was usually possible to place hand-looms on upper storeys; Allison at Thorngate Wynd had dyehouses on the lower floor and weaving shops above, as shown by the details of the buildings described in a mortgage release dated 1837 (Hanby-Holmes 2/10/496) and shown on the left of the engraving by Rock & Co., London, 1863 (fig. 34).

When the Pratts' factory was obliged to close, the notice of sale referred to 'A freehold dwelling house, carpet factory, warehouse and premises in Bridgegate ... The property adjoins the River Tees and much of it is newly built. It comprises Warehouses, Weaving Shops, Dyehouses, Stores, Warping-Rooms ...' (*Darlington & Stockton Times*, 12 April 1851). There were a Steam Engine, Boiler and Dye-pots included as fixtures (fig. 15).

Fig. 31. Raine's Carpet Factory, built in 1839 behind the house shown in fig. 30.

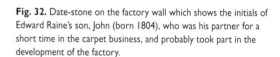

Fig. 32. Date-stone on the factory wall which shows the initials of Edward Raine's son, John (born 1804), who was his partner for a short time in the carpet business, and probably took part in the development of the factory.

Fig. 30. Drawing of a house in Bridgegate, 1982, formerly the home of the owner or manager of Raine's carpet factory which extends behind it (Durham County Council Planning Department).

The premises of Messrs. Monkhouse were of an entirely non-domestic type. From the very early days, they had a factory at the riverside, as shown on the Town Plan of 1827 (fig. 1), and added to this the factory alongside Thorngate. This building, dated 1846, is not dissimilar in proportion from that of Raine's in Bridgegate, being tall and narrow, and extending to three storeys (fig. 35). At about this period, in 1851, according to Walter Shea, Henderson's in Durham City fitted into a shed measuring 161 by 72 feet no fewer than 121 hand-looms, plus some other operations - allowing perhaps ten square yards per loom (Shea, 1984, 61).

A complete contrast to the 1846 factory is provided by Thorngate Mill, built in 1847/8 for the spinning of worsted yarns. An account of Monkhouse's opening ceremony appears in the *Darlington & Stockton Times* of 26 February

1848. It is located on the site of a former saw-mill and race shown on the 1827 Town Plan (fig. 1). This building is much wider than the two already described, and is supported within by iron pillars, seen on the 1996 photograph (fig. 36). The width of the building creates the need for artificial light, at least in the centre of each floor. Gas was available, as shown by Jacob Allison's accounts for 1836 but is not known to have been installed at this mill. The four storeys of Thorngate Mill are connected by a spiral staircase in a projecting tower at the north-east corner, to give easy access from the street, and there are loading facilities to the upper floors from the east frontage. This mill was suitable for a variety of textile production; in the 1870s it was used by a Leeds company, Holroyd and Fieldhouse, who made clothing materials. Mr. Fieldhouse, in traditional fashion, was enumerated in the 1871 census at the nearest house in Thorngate, beside the mill. Some evidence remains in the mill of driving-equipment for the machines, but this is probably much more recent than the carpet-making period.

Fig. 34. Engraving from *Views and Scenery of Barnard Castle* by Rock & Co, London, January 1863, of the area around Thorngate and Thorngate Wynd, from the south bank of the Tees. At the left of the picture are the small three-storey factories in Thorngate Wynd, one dating probably from 1836, the other much older. Just below them is the weir across the Tees, diverting a mill-race behind a 100 metre long embankment to Thorngate Mill, the large building at the far right of the picture.

Dunn's factory was, like the Raine and the 1846 Monkhouse factory, rather tall and narrow, on a cramped site at the westerly end of Bridgegate. This factory is now known only from photographs (fig. 37), but, like the others, was purpose-built. The owner lived a short distance away, across the bridge in Startforth, so that the factory was in no sense a domestic workplace. The factory had five floors, two below road-level with windows towards the river. During demolition of Dunn's factory, several tanks were uncovered, and provided much interest for readers of the local paper, which published an article and photograph (*Teesdale Mercury*, 8 January 1958, fig. 38). The pits were about four feet square and about five feet deep, and were located very close to the river, below the mill. Although there was some suggestion that the pits were part of a drainage system, it appears more likely that they were for Messrs. Dunn's industrial use in preparing the wool yarns.

Fig. 33. Bridgegate Tyres (formerly the factory occupied by Edward Raine), shown in a 1996 photograph of the ground floor. The tyres serve to indicate the dimensions. In about 1835, the Raine family was said to operate 36 looms, (Henderson, 1863), and in 1874, Smith & Powell their successors, had 34 looms (Bartlett, 1978, 209) all for making flat-woven carpets by hand. The factory has two further floors of similar size.

Until the 1830s, dyeing of wool was usually carried out in wood or copper vessels heated by fire; it is known that Ferdinando Ewbank and John Thompson owned such vessels in Barnard Castle in the late eighteenth and early nineteenth centuries (Hanby-Holmes, 3/2/22(1) and 2/7/454). Towards the mid-nineteenth century, one might expect to find a dyer using large cisterns, made from single pieces of quarried stone, and heated by steam. These are well described by Eric Webster in his book on the industries of Halifax (Webster,

Fig. 35. Monkhouse's Factory, Thorngate, Barnard Castle, now converted to houses. A wall-plaque shows the date 1846, and the initials JM & S^S (Joshua Monkhouse & Sons). The arch of a vehicle entrance, now walled-in, is visible at the north end of the frontage. Older pictures of the building show that the arrangement of windows has largely been preserved and that the building always had flues in the gable-ends. The height of the upper storeys would have allowed the use of Jacquard Looms.

Fig. 36. Upper floor at Thorngate Mill, one of the former Monkhouse factories adjacent to the building shown in fig. 35, photographed 1996. It shows the iron pillars used to support a wide, rectangular structure, quite different in proportions from the narrow building shown in figs 31 and 33. Monkhouse's spun some of their own worsted and this building which was opened in February 1848, is believed to be their spinning mill. See also exterior view, fig. 52.

Fig. 37. Dunn's Carpet Factory, Bridgegate, before its demolition in 1958. Production of carpets had ceased in 1888, and the houses which surrounded it were demolished in the 1930's.

Fig. 38. Tanks at Dunn's factory, Bridgegate, Barnard Castle. These were located between the factory wall and the water's edge, and appear to have been used in the dyeing or cleaning of yarn. *Teesdale Mercury* 8 January, 1958.

1970, 34). There seem not to be records of such articles in Barnard Castle, but Pratt's are known to have used equipment known as Robinson's Patent Dyeing Machine, which was offered for sale in 1851(fig. 15) when the company was discontinued (*Darlington & Stockton Times*, 12 April 1851).

Photographs of the Bridgegate-Thorngate industrial area in later Victorian times show how cramped it had all become, with houses and factories cheek-by-jowl. A principal cause of this crowding was the practice of bequeathing property to several sons and daughters, so that the whole was irretrievably divided, as in the case of the Ewbanks' family bequests. Another problem was that owners often lived elsewhere, leasing their properties for the sake of the income. Even if the industry had survived it would have been enormously difficult and expensive to rebuild for its needs in the later nineteenth century.

Plate 11. Small fragment of flat-woven carpeting, Kidderminster type, probably Barnard Castle, 1830-50, showing both sides of the reversible double cloth. This small piece was recently discovered in a dolls' house of about 1830, which came from Stubb House, Barnard Castle and was given to The Bowes Museum in 1940. Cat. No. 6

Plate 12. Point paper design for carpeting registered by Monkhouse, Whitfield & Co., Barnard Castle, 13 May 1845, no. 27503. Gouache on squared paper (16 to inch) sheet size: 58 x 38 cm. This over-elaborate, ambitious design in at least 13 colours seems to be a wild flight of fancy for the Barnard Castle manufacturers, and was perhaps registered with an exhibition in mind.

Plate 13. Point paper design for carpeting, registered by Richard Dunn, Barnard Castle, 9 August 1851, no. 80103. Inscribed in ink on border 'Richard Dunn, Carpet Manufacturer, Barnard Castle no. 348'. Gouache on squared paper (16 to inch) printed '50 x 40 Designs' '8 by 6 No. 1' sheet size: 14.5 x 15.5 cm. A bold design with a border of curled leaves and a seaweed type design as the body pattern.

Plate 14. Edward Raine's carpet mill, built 1839, seen from the south bank of the River Tees in 1996. The door in the gable-end allowed access to the river by way of a short flight of stone steps, later demolished. The outline of a blocked second door is visible above the existing one.

CHAPTER 6

THE WORKFORCE

The workforce employed in Barnard Castle was, to a large degree, local. Weaving is traditionally a family business, and whole families were engaged in the industry. This practice might extend over several generations, as in the Etherington, Wigham, Cheesebrough and Morton families. Members of families whose father was not a carpet weaver were unlikely to enter the industry, whether it was flourishing or declining, so that it remained very traditional throughout the period of its existence.

Manufacturers whose businesses had grown would employ a manager. Mr. William Mitchell, for example, was manager at Pratt's. The census return for 1851 shows that he was a Scot by birth, perhaps from another carpet weaving centre. Before coming to Barnard Castle about 1845, he had lived in Durham City. He was married and had young children and no doubt expected the move to Pratt's to bring him professional advancement. Instead, he found himself responsible for showing potential purchasers around the factory as it was put up for sale by John Pratt's Executors in 1851; one can guess the disappointment he must have felt. Monkhouse's factory shows some evidence of a system of intermediate management. The carpet department had Sandy Lockhead as foreman, and prominent weavers were Mr. Richmond, Mr. Eales and Mr. Harris. The mill mechanic was Mr. Longbottom, and Mr. Mackay and Mr. Preston were well-known workmen. All these employees were named in the *Darlington & Stockton Times* of 26 February 1848, as they made significant contributions to the banquet at the opening of the new worsted mill.

A clear division of labour was apparent between the sexes, the men taking the physically more demanding tasks, which as it happened, often meant the more skilled tasks. Fathers and older sons would be weavers, younger sons might work as 'drawboys' at Brussels looms, and women or girls would be employed as 'winders'. Warping was done by either men or women. Dyeing was a man's occupation. Quite a number of women and youths would be known as 'factory girl' or 'factory boy' or would tell the census enumerator just that they 'worked at the mill'. Until Monkhouse's developed a fleece-to-fabric operation and employed worsted spinners, usually women, the manufacturers bought in yarn and concentrated on dyeing, weaving and finishing. Some idea of the number of carpet-workers in the town can be formed from the census returns, tabulated below:

Table: Census Years x Numbers of Carpet-workers

Year	1841	1851	1861	1871	1881	1891
Carpet weavers	226	272	46	58	44	33
Part-time weavers			3	-	-	3
Weaver apprentices			3	3	-	-
Other male workers	26	30	1	3	1	2
Total of men employed	252	302	53	64	45	38
Women (winders etc.)	41	63	6	6+	6	5
Total of carpet workers	293	365	59	70	51	43

(+ is an estimate. It is difficult by this time to distinguish carpet workers from woollen and tweed workers).

When the carpet industry was at its busiest, it contributed to the economic welfare of up to one quarter of the population of Barnard Castle. In 1841, a total of 877 people from families of carpet-weavers depended wholly or partly on the carpet industry. In 1851, this had risen to 970 people (even though by the latter date each carpet-worker supported fewer dependents). In 1841, there were 545 dependents, but by 1851, the number had fallen to 479, about half the family members. This proportion of half-working, half-dependent, was maintained for the rest of the century. Another development which occurred in the second half of the century was that members of weaver households became more inclined to seek work outside the carpet industry. These family members tended to be semi-dependent people, such as older children, other relatives or lodgers and numbered 49 in 1841, and 126 in 1851. After the mid century, there was little evidence of unskilled men or women working in the carpet trade, and the practice of apprenticing boys had died out. Drawboys, of whom there had been a dozen in 1851, were no longer needed, indicating possibly a decline in the trade for Brussels carpets.

Among the general workforce, there were always a few who had arrived in the town from other carpet-making areas, such as Kidderminster, the West Riding and Scotland, as well as from Darlington and Durham City, and later in the period, from Ireland. The census returns of 1841 and 1851 show that the proportion of immigrant weavers grew. In 1841, 8% (19/226) of the weavers aged twelve or over had been born elsewhere; by 1851 this had risen to almost 18% (48/272), and by 1861 to almost 23% (12/53). Apart from 1871, when there were very few immigrants indeed (three among sixty weavers), the proportion of immigrants remained at about the same level; in 1881 it was 19% (8/43) and in 1891 24% (8/33). Men seeking work must often have encountered hardship. One Edward Bolland, a married man with two children, left his family in Heckmondwike (another carpet-weaving centre) in the West Riding of Yorkshire, before Christmas 1891 to come to Barnard Castle. In May 1892, already ill, probably from consumption, he cut his own throat with a small table knife (*Teesdale Mercury*, 25 May 1892).

Until the 1870s workers were apparently employed from the age of about twelve until they were well over seventy, but after that date, weavers were generally aged between fifteen and the late sixties. Children between about four and twelve were usually 'scholars', although it is not certain that they actually attended school. Boys were more likely than girls to start work at twelve, while girls stayed a little longer at school and then spent a year or two at home before going to work at the factory. Girls often worked in the flax industry as an alternative to the carpet mill. Many of the young workers came from needy families. Often, the census shows that there was a widowed mother, a sister with an illegitimate child, or an elderly parent in the same household. It was not particularly common for married women to work in the carpet industry unless they were childless, the children had grown up, or there was a daughter to keep house.

Welfare of employees became a popular development in nineteenth century industry, but there is only fragmentary evidence of it in Barnard Castle, where employers were less prosperous. Nevertheless, it is apparent that from the very foundation of the carpet industry (See Chapter 1) employers were inclined to concern themselves with matters which were for the common good. John Pratt was active in Public Health during the cholera epidemic, and Richard Dunn was often associated with local government as it developed out of the Public Health Boards during the century. J.C. Monkhouse was interested in railway provision. Of the individual companies, Monkhouse's is probably the only one known to have begun some sort of welfare provision. 'Weavers' Footings' (sums of money paid as premiums by new employees) were paid into a benefit fund to provide death benefit and other reliefs. (*Darlington & Stockton Times*, 13 October and 11 November 1849). A Sick Society was formed in 1852 which for a payment of tenpence halfpenny a month provided the services of a doctor and a weekly sickness allowance for one year (*Darlington & Stockton Times*, 3 April 1852). This could have been most necessary; in April 1852, 'a son of George Metcalf got entangled in the machinery by some means and his legs (were) dreadfully cut. He lingered until 2nd instant (May) when he died from the effects of his injury' (*Darlington & Stockton Times*, 6 May 1854).

Wages were controlled by the employers in conference. When Richard Dunn in 1850 refused to pay wages at the established local level, his workers went on strike for five months. The strike cost the workers £140 to conduct, but was 'unusually peaceful ... not a single row or breach of the peace having taken place'. The strike ended when Dunn was persuaded at a meeting of the masters on October 11th to pay the right wages (*Darlington & Stockton Times*, 2 November 1850). Wages varied from time to time, and according to the work done. Piece rates of about ten shillings per length of carpet, equivalent to about a week's work, were paid by Jacob Allison in the 1820s, probably to workers based at home. By the mid-century, a skilled weaver in a factory might earn twenty-five shillings a week (Chapter 8). Women, in ancillary occupations within the factory, and young workers, would be paid much less, perhaps half the men's rates. Men paid 'footings' to join the workforce, and apprentices, or their parents, paid premiums (*Darlington & Stockton Times*, 27 October 1849 and 3 November 1849).

It seems that most employers kept grocers' shops, which were probably used by the workers. Certainly, Pigot's *Directory* of 1834 lists among the grocers John Ramshaw, John Pratt and Edward Raine, all in Bridgegate. The Monkhouse family had connections with the food trade through Joshua himself who was a grocer, and his son J.R.Monkhouse who was a provision dealer at Bowes for part of his working life. The Truck Act of 1831 prohibited 'the Payment, in certain Trades, of Wages in Goods, or otherwise than in the current Coin of the Realm', but until the Act was amended in 1887, employers could lawfully stipulate where wages might be spent. It is interesting to note that in the leadmining industry in Upper Teesdale the workmen, assisted by their employer the London Lead Company had begun one of the earliest and probably the first, co-operative society in 1842 to provide flour and, later, general groceries.

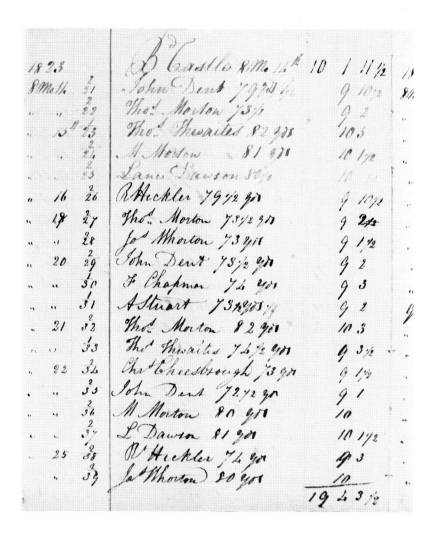

Fig. 39. Entries from Jacob Allison's Wages Book, 1823, believed to be in his own writing. They clearly relate to business at Barnard Castle. The left-hand column shows the date in Quaker style, month first, and the next column, a payment number, 21 to 39, beneath a number 1 or 2, of which the use is not certain. Next come the weavers' names. Most of the men can be traced in local parochial records, and belong to established weaver families. The precise length of each piece is shown and in the right-hand column, the piece-payment to the weaver, the rate being three-halfpence a yard. A weaver might earn about nine or ten shillings a week, depending on his work-rate. Allison carries forward the total payment until the year end. It is likely that the weavers worked at home at this date (Mrs. M. Hamilton).

CHAPTER 7

THE LIFE AND WORK OF JACOB ALLISON - A CASE STUDY

Although Jacob Allison (active 1825-38) was one of the smallest manufacturers in the town, his account-books have survived, providing an insight into day-to-day operations in a carpet manufactory which is not available for the larger firms. It is probably reasonable to assume that much of Allison's activity resembled that of his fellow-manufacturers, so that this account of his operations is offered as an example of contemporary practice at the time when carpet weaving was expanding in Barnard Castle.

Allison has left four books: an Order Book 1823 to 1828, showing goods ordered and dispatched; a Cash Book 1823 to 1852 showing many types of transactions, including wages paid from 1823 to 1827 to named individuals; a Day Book showing debtors and creditors from 1830 to 1850 with chronological arrangement of transactions; and an indexed Register of Debtors and Creditors for 1836 onwards. It is emphasised that the existing books do not rep-

Fig. 40. Notice of sale of carpet manufactory and other property, Barnard Castle, 1835. This is clear evidence of Jacob Allison's situation in 1835, when his landlady died, and helps to explain the developments recorded in his accounts in 1836. It also supports the view gained from the accounts that Allison was conducting a combined dyeing and weaving operation at Thorngate Wynd. Miss Ewbank was a relative of Allison's late landlady. Parker Crosby (a former cotton manufacturer) and John Gibson were relatives by marriage. The property was sold to yet another relative, Henry Ewbank. (Mr. R.J. Hanby-Holmes)

resent complete accounts. Stocks are not listed, there is no register of assets, and of course, details of bank accounts are unknown, so that it is sometimes difficult to ascertain Allison's profitability, or to find out the details of his activities in business. The inside cover of the Cash Book shows it was purchased in Barnard Castle from Atkinson's booksellers.

Jacob Allison was the youngest son of Joseph and Ann Allison, of Cotherstone, a village four miles from Barnard Castle. The Allison family could trace its descent in this area from Elizabethan times, and owned some land in and around the village. Joseph Allison (1751-1837) was probably a farmer; Baine's *Directory of North Riding of Yorkshire*, 1822 shows his elder surviving son, John (1793-1851) as a farmer, and Jacob as a stuff manufacturer in Cotherstone. The Allisons were committed members of the Society of Friends; indeed, Joseph had been one of the Trustees of the new Meeting House built at Cotherstone in 1796 (Quaker

Meeting Minutes). Jacob had received a good education, including book-keeping. He was certainly at Barnard Castle by 1823, when he began to pay weavers by the piece (fig. 39), but it is not known whether he employed the men at a factory or commissioned them to work at their homes. It may have been the latter arrangement, because payment of rent for premises in Thorngate Wynd began in 1827, as the piecework payments died away and were replaced by wage payments. The manufactory that Allison rented was owned by the Ewbank family, but leased out, for the life-long benefit of Jane, the widow of William Ewbank (died 1820). The Ewbanks had been engaged in the textile industry some forty years earlier, so that their property, situated close to the river in Barnard Castle, was probably quite suited to Jacob's needs. The site contained a messe (dwelling) and dyehouses, together with a drying ground, and four cottages in Thorngate Wynd which were tenanted by the weaver families of Race and Smith. 'Allison developed his business here at a steady pace for some years. The 1827 Town Plan (fig. 1) shows a building at the end of Thorngate Wynd, bordering the river, as the property of Mrs. Jane Brookes (formerly Mrs. Ewbank) and this is likely to be the manufactory. The Poll Book shows that in 1832 Allison lived in Thorngate, in a house owned by George Atkinson, a relative of his landlady.

Parson & White's *Directory,* 1827, shows that a company known as J. & J. Allison was established in Thorngate Wynd at

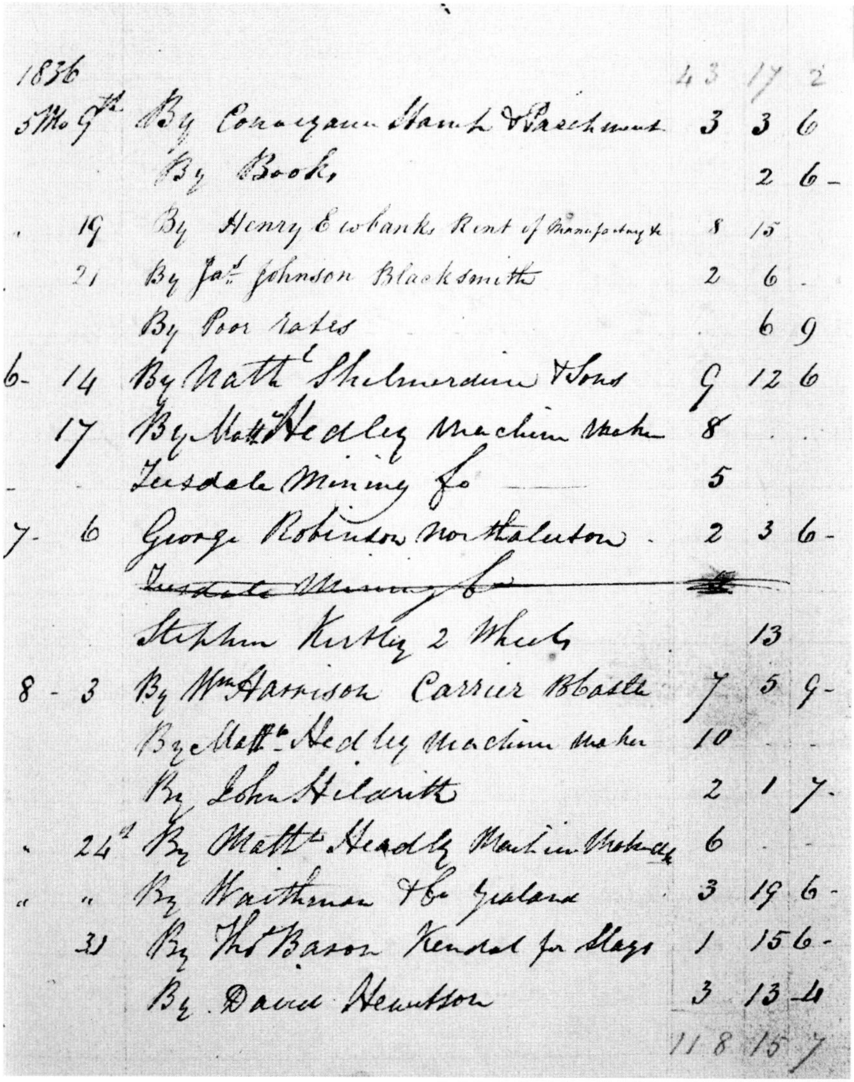

1836		43	17	2
5 Mo 9th	By Conveyance Stamp & Parchment	3	3	6
	By Book,		2	6 -
19	By Henry Ewbank Rent of Manufactory &c	8	15	
21	By Jas. Johnson Blacksmith	2	6	.
	By Poor rates	.	6	9
6 - 14	By Nathl Shelmerdine & Sons	9	12	6
17	By Matt Hedley Machine Maker	8	.	.
	Teesdale Mining Co	5		
7 - 6	George Robinson Northallerton	2	3	6 -
	~~Teesdale Mining Co~~	~~5~~		
	Stephen Kirtley 2 Wheels		13	
8 - 3	By Wm Harrison Carrier B Castle	7	5	9 -
	By Mattw Hedley Machine Maker	10	.	.
	By John Hewitt	2	1	7 -
24	By Mattw Headly Machine Maker	6	.	.
"	By Waithman & Co Yealand	3	19	6 -
31	By Thos Bason Kendal for Slays	1	15	6 -
	By David Hewitson	3	13	4
		118	15	7

Fig. 41. Entries from Allison's Cash Book, May to August 1836. Allison is buying new looms, slays and wheels, and paying a new landlord, Henry Ewbank. He is carrying out a property deal, with formal conveyance, and also a mining transaction, possibly a speculation in the lead industry. Shelmerdine supplied chemicals, Hewitson was a carrier based at Kendal, and Waithman of Yealand supplied canvas, probably for wrapping carpet pieces in transit. The third, fourth and fifth entries are made by Allison's wife, Mary. (Mrs. M. Hamilton)

that date. It is likely that the partner was John, Jacob's brother. In 1828/9, Pigot's *Directory* shows the business bearing the name of Jacob alone. Darlington Quaker Meeting minutes of 1829 show that John Allison left the area, and was accepted into membership of a meeting at Newcastle. It appears that Jacob bought John out of his house at Cotherstone and possibly also out of the partnership. Between August 1829 and December 1838, he paid John just over £400 in cash, most if it for 'the house'.

As the Thorngate Wynd manufactory was not Jacob's own property, he was in a very vulnerable position when in July 1835, Mrs. Brookes died, and the property was offered for sale with Allison himself as one of the tenants (Hanby-Holmes 2/7/449-451, - fig. 40).

In November 1835 the property was bought by Henry Ewbank, a relative of the late owner, who raised a mortgage of some £370 as the purchase cost (Hanby-Holmes 2/10/508). Briefly, he became Allison's landlord. One might wonder why Allison did not himself purchase the buildings. It is not known whether he made any attempt to do so, but as things turned out, he was perhaps fortunate to have kept out of this responsibility.

In April 1836 Allison married Mary Graham, from Hethergill in Cumberland. She, too, was a Friend, who had received a formal education. She was able to help with the accounts, her handwriting being clearly identified by comparison with the family's commonplace book, which is retained at the Durham County Record Office (SF/Co/PM8/9).

During 1836, Allison's books show a good deal of expenditure on the manufactory (fig. 41). That year, many items in the accounts show the purchase of equipment, usually by cash. Local firms, Smith's of Barnard Castle and Atkinson's of Darlington, were paid for machines at £6 each, or £7 with weights. Matthew Hedley, machine maker, was paid £8 or £6, and Stephen Kirtley, a local woodworker, was paid for shuttles. Local men were also paid for glass, and for glazing, for bricks, for attention to a fireplace, and also for whitewashing the manufactory. Finally, a new plate was acquired - whether for the door or for letter headings is not known. In January 1837 grates were bought for the dyehouse. These appear to be the sorts of items a tenant might provide, because they are on the whole not fixtures.

On 12 March 1837 Joseph Allison, Jacob's father, died. This might have been important in influencing Jacob's plans for the future. Allison's last rent for the manufactory in Thorngate Wynd was paid in May 1837. By the autumn of 1837, when the next rent would have been payable, Richard Atkin, who had been a partner of John Winskill as carpet weavers in a neighbouring street of Barnard Castle, had formed a partnership with John Thompson, a butcher. These two men arranged to take over the property, with a much-increased mortgage, amounting to £770 altogether (Hanby-Holmes 2/10/508). Legal papers show that the manufactory building had been extended to two separate units, each offering dyehouses to the lower floor, and weaving rooms on the upper storeys. Allison was occupying a cottage on the same site (Hanby-Holmes 2/10/496).

It is not at present known exactly when Jacob Allison left Thorngate Wynd. It is, however, clear that he continued through 1838 and 1839 to operate as a manufacturer of carpets, producing to the value of perhaps £2,000 annually. This quantity he might have been able to achieve at Cotherstone, employing, say, four weavers, and selling the pieces for about £10 to £13 each. He need not have rented special premises, as the weavers could have worked at home, in the old-fashioned way, or even in some building owned by the Allison family. It was perhaps as well that Allison had an alternative way of life open to him, and did not become too closely dependent on Atkin and Thompson. In January, 1838 Richard Atkin died. This caused an immediate financial crisis, as his partnership with Thompson was so very recently formed and very much dependent on borrowed money. At the end of 1839 the Thompson-Atkins venture had completely failed, and the factory was put up for sale (fig 42).

From about 1837/8 Allison's accounts show an increasing element of personal expenditure, including housekeeping expenses, doctor's and funeral bills, personal travel and small household repairs. Allison also traded in the occasional farm animal, and in lime and in animal foodstuffs, and paid various taxes, probably in relation to the family property.

In 1840 the position is clear - Allison is named in White's *Directory* as a carpet manufacturer at Cotherstone, which was at that time in North Yorkshire. Allison brought with him to Cotherstone the weavers Dobson and Heighley, who had previously lived at Barnard Castle. Wages payments suggest a very small payroll, perhaps only one or two weavers, producing up to two pieces a week. After the carpet venture declined, he engaged in the tweed trade, which is recorded in his books for the year 1849, but as late as May 1850 the Day Book shows a consignment of eight pieces of Kidderminster carpet to London. Allison also developed his work as a lead-mine agent, his main occupation as declared in the censuses of 1851 and 1861. He died in 1868, and is buried in the yard of the Quaker Meeting House at Cotherstone.

Jacob Allison made a variety of flat-woven carpets - Kidderminster in several qualities, Venetian in several qualities, some Damask, and small quantities of twill and kersey weaves, usually for stairs. He also made hearthrugs and some mats suitable for interior doorways. Some examples of entries in the order book illustrate the scope of the undertaking:

Example 1 Dated 11 July 1828

7/11	Thos Friend Bp. Wearmouth	
I Ps 4/4 Kiddr Comm		844 @ 2/-
I Ps ' ' '		162 @ 2/-
I Ps 4/4 Super		10 @ 2/10
I Ps 5/8 Strip		40 @ 1/3
I do 2/4 do		40 @ 1/-

This order, to a shop or warehouse in a North-eastern coastal town, shows that various grades and widths of Kidderminster carpet were produced, for a variety of locations in the house. The expression 'Ps' means 'piece', (this would be about 90 yards in length) and the fraction following shows the width, 4/4 being the maximum, one yard, and the other proportionally. The design number is 844. The prices per running yard vary according to the width and the quality of the carpet; a piece of 844 would cost about £9.

Example 2 Dated 21 August 1828

1828 Orders received		When sent off
8/21st	J.S. Bassett, London	
I Ps No 1	4/4 Chocolate, Green & Red	9/24
I ' '	Green gd as 844 and Red	10/3
I Ps No 2	Chocolate gd same as pattern	11/12
I ' No 3	Green gd Red, Yellow & White	10/17
I ' '	Blue gd Red, Yellow & white	10/31
I ' No 4	Blue & Red as pattern	10/31
I ' '	Green gd as 844 & Red	11/12

This entry is particularly informative. John Swinford Bassett of Number 2, Love Lane, and 34 Wood Street (from January 1830) was a proprietor of a Woollen Cloth and Carpet

Warehouse, recorded in Pigot's 1839 *London Directory*. Bassett is ordering Kidderminster carpet from patterns, and requesting complete pieces rather than carpet cut to order. He was therefore taking some risk. Allison was able to create variety by weaving the same style in different ground (gd) colours. The date of despatch is expressed in the traditional Quaker style, where 10/31 means 31 October and it shows a delivery date of six to twelve weeks.

Special orders were sometimes received. In June 1829, Bassett bought Dutch carpet in several colourways: in green, drab, black and white; in green, blue, red and scarlet; and in green, drab, black and scarlet. In April 1829, George Nicholson of 30 Aldgate High Street, London, a linen draper, bought Venetian carpet in 4/4 width, style No. 10. He wanted 'three squares of Green, the middle pea green and 3 squares of scarlet'. About the same time, Messrs. William & Jonathan Kynaston, of Lad Lane, Cheapside, Woollen Warehouse proprietors, wanted two pieces of No 6 with green ground; to be made light, with thirteen ounces per square yard, for which they were charged twenty pence per yard. This is a weight of fabric more usual in tailoring or furnishing; perhaps Kynaston wanted it for hangings, or upholstery.

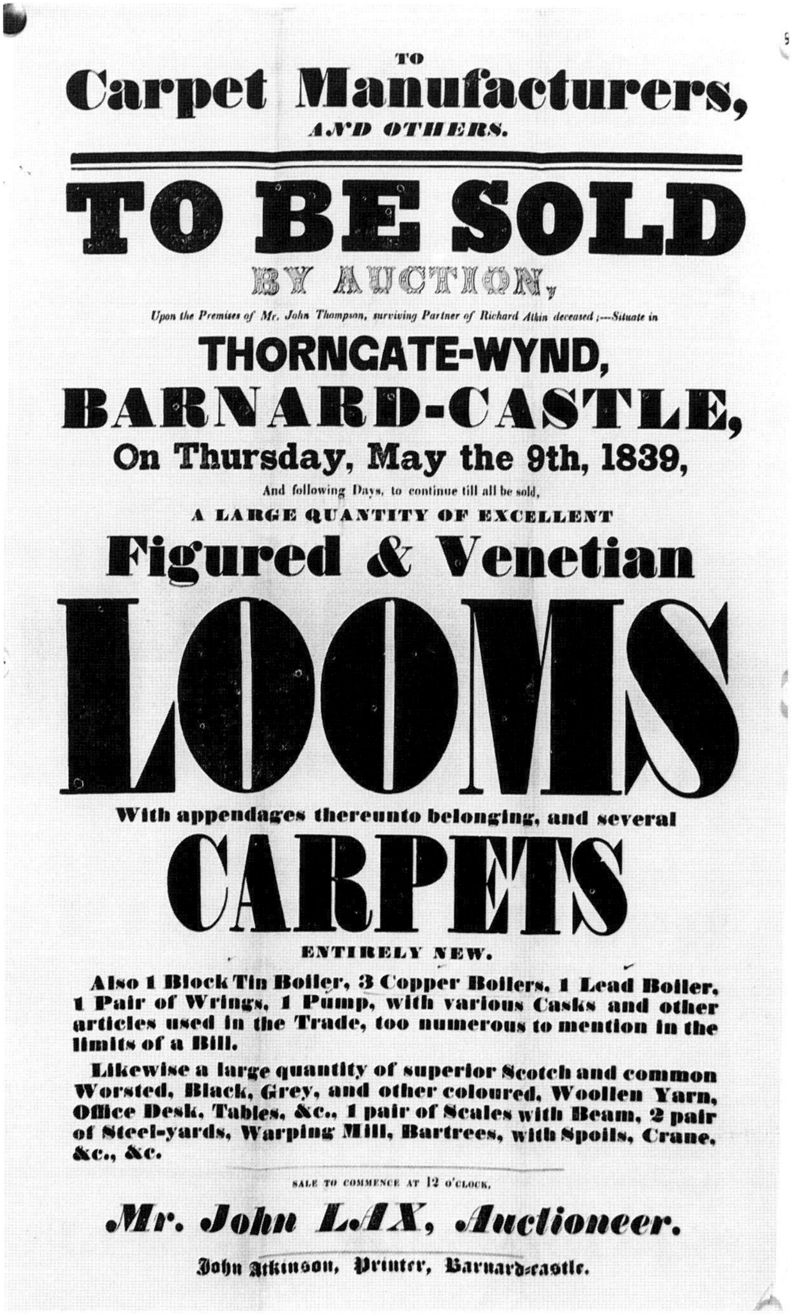

TO
Carpet Manufacturers,
AND OTHERS.

TO BE SOLD
BY AUCTION,

Upon the Premises of Mr. John Thompson, surviving Partner of Richard Atkin deceased ;—Situate in

THORNGATE-WYND,
BARNARD-CASTLE,

On Thursday, May the 9th, 1839,

And following Days, to continue till all be sold,

A LARGE QUANTITY OF EXCELLENT

Figured & Venetian
LOOMS

With appendages thereunto belonging, and several

CARPETS

ENTIRELY NEW.

Also 1 Block Tin Boiler, 3 Copper Boilers, 1 Lead Boiler, 1 Pair of Wrings, 1 Pump, with various Casks and other articles used in the Trade, too numerous to mention in the limits of a Bill.

Likewise a large quantity of superior Scotch and common Worsted, Black, Grey, and other coloured, Woollen Yarn, Office Desk, Tables, &c., 1 pair of Scales with Beam, 2 pair of Steel-yards, Warping Mill, Bartrees, with Spoils, Crane, &c., &c.

SALE TO COMMENCE AT 12 O'CLOCK.

Mr. John LAX, Auctioneer.

John Atkinson, Printer, Barnard-castle.

Fig. 42. Poster dated 1839, and printed by Atkinson's, who from 1854, published the local newspaper, the *Teesdale Mercury*. The auction was occasioned by a bankruptcy, and gives an insight into the variety of goods being produced. The bankrupt partnership, Thompson and Atkin, may, according to Henderson (1863), have had as many as sixty looms. (Mr. R.J. Hanby-Holmes)

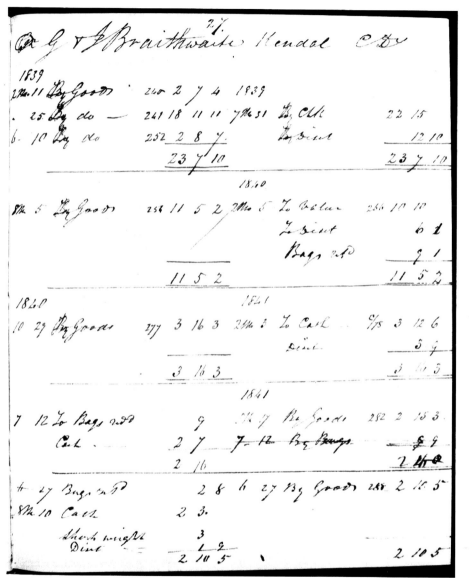

Fig. 43. Page from Allison's supplier and customer ledger, showing several years' entries for George and Isaac Braithwaite of Kendal, his suppliers of dyestuffs. Allison sometimes balanced his accounts at the half-year, instead of annually. He paid Braithwaite by cash, and often the transactions are cross-referenced with the Day Book, which lists the items bought. This series of entries shows the volume of business declining during the years at Cotherstone. (Mrs. M. Hamilton)

In two particular periods, 1824 to 1829, and again in 1830 to 1834, Allison's accounts sometimes show the colours as well as the pattern numbers of the carpets sold to a London warehouse. Thus, a useful, but not exhaustive, record exists, indicating a degree of change in fashion. In the earlier period, twenty-six different designs, nearly all Kidderminster, were manufactured, and further variety created by offering several colourways of many of them. Each year, up to five new designs appeared. The most common colour mentioned, in combination, or as a main colour, was green, which was three times more common than chocolate, and four times more common than blue. Yellow, red and drab were used as main colours, but were uncommon. In combination, scarlet, black, white and pink all appeared occasionally.

In the later period, many of the same patterns continued to be used. Between twelve and fourteen different Kidderminster patterns, and up to five Venetian patterns would be available each year, but the selection changed quite frequently as some patterns were dropped and others introduced. Of the twenty-five patterns used in the five-year period only four were used in every year, and many were mentioned in only one year's accounts. Colours remained similar to those of the earlier period, but chocolate and green were now almost equally frequent. Drab (a light grey-brown, very popular at the time, possibly used by Allison to indicate undyed wool) was the second most common and blue and yellow relatively rare. Other rare colours were red, crimson, scarlet, lilac, black, white, brown and pea green. Combinations were found in blue/drab, black/red, drab/white and red/green, sometimes in a damask weave.

Allison's Cash Book and Order Books show that up to about 1835, he purchased much wool and ready-made yarn in the North Pennine area. Allison contracted out spinning to mills as far away as Howgill, near Sedbergh, and Copelandbeck, near Appleby, both in Cumbria. He also bought yarn - often worsted - from a company at Burnley, Lancashire, named Massey, and from two companies in Darlington: Henry Pease (worsted) and Ianson Toulmin & Ord (linen). He bought specialized materials from the West Riding of Yorkshire, especially from Halliday & Rhodes of Heckmondwike, including silk noil, tow yarns and silk yarn. The latter was already dyed in yellow, red, green or chocolate.

Throughout Allison's working life, he bought dyestuffs mainly from George & Isaac Braithwaite of Kendal (fig. 43), who had supplied weavers in Barnard Castle since 1739. A large order placed on 8 February 1830 included Redwood, Peachwood, Inca Bark, Logwood (already rasped), Indigo, Cochineal and Cream of Tartar. A few weeks later, 3 May, Allison bought White Argot, Lac Dye, Grain Tin and Cochineal, and some time later, on 9 August, he bought

Rasped Logwood, Fustic, Cudbear and Cochineal (See Dye Analysis, Appendix II). It is interesting to see that other chemicals, for example mordants, and also soaps, used in scouring of wool, were bought from the traditional chemical production areas near the mouth of the Tees. In 1838 he dealt with Robert Wilson of Egglescliffe and Sanders & Weatherall of Stockton in buying a variety of scouring and mordant agents, such as soap, spirits of salt and vitriol.

Allison's cash expenditure for the years 1830 and 1838 shows how his business dealings had changed. In 1830 he spent by cash some £1003, and in 1838 about £1405, £713 in the first half and £692 in the second; these totals include expenditure on the textile business of £908 in 1830 and £856 in 1838, suggesting that he was developing other means of livelihood. In round terms, the spend was as follows:

Jacob Allison - Expenditure by Cash in 1830 and 1838

	1830	1838
Wages	£325	£279
Yarn/Spinning	£301	£470
Wool	£176	nil
Rents	£34	5/-
Chemicals/Dyes	£28	£60
Carriage	£22	£26
Paper/office sundries	£11	12/-
Personal travel	£8	£11
Insurance	£3	£4
Poor Rates	2/6	£3
Postages	nil	£2
Approximate Totals	£908	£826

The Day Book for 1830 shows raw materials to the value of £929 in 1830 and £547 in 1838, as shown below:

Jacob Allison - Materials Recorded in Day Book during 1830 and 1838

	1830	1838
Yarn and Spinning to the value of	£580	£502
Chemicals and dyes to the value of	£262	£45
Wool to the value of	£51	nil
Linen and Canvas	£36	nil
Totals	£929	£547

The pattern of supply, as well as the value, changed between the two dates. By 1838, very large quantities of yarn were bought from a small number of suppliers in the West Riding, displacing the more local and smaller farmers and spinners. If Dutch carpet was not being made, then fibres other than wool may not have been required.

In 1830, Allison's twenty-eight commercial customers, in London and in the North-East, ordered 317 pieces of carpet and sixty-two rugs. The sizes of orders varied widely. The biggest orders came from J.S.Bassett, who purchased sixty items, mainly Dutch carpet, Thomas Robson of Sunderland (twenty-four items, mainly rugs), James Deacon & Sons, Scotch and Irish Linen Factors of 4 Lad Lane and 1 Clement's Court, London (forty-one items), Halleby & Carter of 57 Coleman Street, London (twenty-three items) and Blythe Inglis Carpet Warehouse of 9 Old Fish Street, London (seventeen items). There was quite a variety of products. Many orders were for Dutch, and a few for Super Dutch. There were Kidderminster pieces in Common, Fine, Super and Superfine qualities as well as Leightweight [sic]. Damask, Venetian and Fine Venetian were less common. Stair carpet was sometimes described as Twill, once as Kersey, but more usually just as plain Stair. Hearthrugs, either figured or plain and door mats, seemed to go to local traders, sometimes as in the case of George Binns of Sunderland, to High Street shops. On the face of it, the year 1830 seems likely to have been profitable, but with heavy reliance on only a small number of customers, Allison was not guaranteed to be secure. He played for safety by making to order, and besides the carpet trade, still had interests in stuffs and plaids for local tailors.

In 1838 Allison turned out possibly as much as £2,000 worth - say about 175 pieces - of carpet, all Kidderminster. The prices were 2/- to 3/- per yard, or £9 to £13 per piece, an increase at the top of the range since 1830, and the number of pieces made was much smaller. The range of carpets had reduced in the intervening time; in 1831 Allison had sent to London four types of Kidderminster, five types of Venetian, three types of Dutch, two types of Damask, three types of stair-carpet and some hearthrugs, a total of one hundred and twenty-three pieces. By 1837 ninety out of ninety-nine pieces were Fine or Super Kidderminster. In 1838 there were only three London agents, handling about £850 worth of goods. The majority of the production went to large provincial towns, such as Liverpool, Leeds, Nottingham, York, Stockport, Stockton and Warrington, and also to Penrith, but not to Tyneside. This provincial trade accounted for about £1035 worth of goods to about thirty customers. There were also a few local domestic purchasers, such as the owner of Wodencroft, a boarding-school at Cotherstone.

A typical order to London agents T. & M. Hutchinson dated 14 October 1838:

To goods on Commission

I ps	4/4	Super Kiddr		43	88 yds
I ps	4/4	do	do	65	87 1/2
I ps	4/4	do	do	45	88
I ps	4/4	do	do	84	87
I ps	4/4	Fine	do	55	89
I ps	4/4	do	do	55	88 1/2
		per the 'Emerald Isle'			

No prices are mentioned here, but there are several different pattern-numbers, and two different qualities of carpet. Commission was 2.5%. The lengths of the pieces are rather varied, as they had been many years before, probably because of the hand-made nature of the fabric. Transport was by sea, still probably from Stockton. Reliance on sea transport may account for sales in cities such as Liverpool, Belfast and Dublin.

An output worth about £2,000 was probably sufficient, as otherwise Allison would have been unlikely to continue the venture. A complete assessment of the situation however cannot be made from available evidence. It is not apparent, for instance, what funds Allison needed to pay for business premises, or what working capital he had raised.

The accounts show much involvement with Backhouse's Bank which handled payments from distant customers. Frequent use of acceptances and bills, especially in paying yarn suppliers, may suggest some difficulty, or may merely be the most practical way of handing over the payments. The customer ledger suggests that most provincial customers paid fairly promptly, as Allison received about £960 from them in the one year in respect of orders priced at £1033. The London trade was much slower to pay; Hutchinson's paid £412 in the year, and charged commission and postage. At the end of 1838, the balance owing to suppliers Halliday & Rhodes had risen from £93 to £118, but Allison apparently had settled smaller debts by cash, fairly quickly.

Allison's carpet trade dwindled away after about 1839, but the accounts, which become increasingly fragmentary, show that carpet was still produced as late as 1850. On 8 May that year, Allison sold T. & M. Hutchinson stair and twill carpet priced as low as 10d a yard (1/4 a square yard): Not surprisingly, Allison had by then diverted his weavers' principal efforts into the making of tweed instead.

Fourteen years after this T. & M. Hutchinson decided to begin the manufacture of carpets on their own account. They set up a factory at Barnes Cray in Kent recruiting as manager an experienced employee of Crossley and Sons. Despite the problems caused by being remote from other carpet making towns and having no local tradition of the trade the firm had some early success and in 1869 had twenty-one Brussels power looms. By 1885 the venture had failed. (Bartlett, 1979, 71)

Fig. 44. This lithograph by P. Naumann, late nineteenth century, shows the concentration of industrial buildings along the north bank of the river.

CHAPTER 8

LIVING CONDITIONS

In the first half of the nineteenth century most working class people in Barnard Castle were employed in the factories, despite the town's traditional role as an agricultural centre and market town. In 1821 a total of 626 families derived their income from factory work, in contrast to the 94 families who depended on agriculture; by the middle of the century 70% of the town's population of 4,351 people were manually employed (Ranger, 1850, 5). The majority of them worked in riverside factories (fig. 44). Not all of these factories produced carpets; there were others which produced woollen goods of various kinds, and a flax mill was situated at Bridge End on the south bank of the Tees (fig. 45).

Whatever particular trade they were engaged in, however, all the workers lived in the same area of the town and in very similar conditions to each other. Their living accommodation was over-crowded, ill-ventilated, and lacking in decent sanitary arrangements. Four-fifths of the weavers lived in large houses which had been divided into one-room tenements, each accommodating one family or another group of people who had agreed to share a room (*Parliamentary*

Fig. 45. This oil painting dating probably from the early years of this century shows workers crossing the County bridge, going from the flax mill on the south bank of the river towards their homes in the town. One or two generations earlier a similar procession might have been seen going to their work in the carpet factories on the north bank.

Report on Poor Law Union, 1841). Several of the houses had been quite dignified residences of well-to-do families who had lived in the riverside streets before industrial buildings had risen there. The richer families had then moved out, and the houses were sub-divided into tenements for which the workers paid rent.

Behind these large houses were yards which were entered through a narrow alleyway in the ground floor of the house. Other workers lived up these yards, in former stables and other outbuildings. Most of these yards were in Thorngate and Bridgegate, and were sunless and airless - particularly on the north side of Bridgegate where the yards terminated at the high rocky cliff on top of which stood the castle. Space for housing near the factories was so limited that some houses were built against the cliff high above the street and were reached by sloping paths and flights of stone steps. The home of Robert Johnson Cain (fig. 46) described in his obituary as 'one of the most expert yard-wide carpet weavers in England' (*Teesdale Mercury,* 1924) was perched in this fashion (fig. 47) overlooking the factories. Other yards were in the Market

Place, and some in the Horse Market. There were over seventy yards altogether.

The sanitary arrangements for the people who lived either in the large houses or the outbuildings were woefully inadequate, owing to so many people living in accommodation designed for far fewer (Ranger, 1850, 9-10). In one yard, for example, called Swinburne's (or Peart's) Yard, there was only one privy for the use of thirty-five people, fifteen of whom were children. Some houses in this yard were three storeys high, reached by a passage that was less than six feet wide. In another yard, Old Priory Yard, which was a *cul de sac*, there was one privy for sixty-five people (fig. 54).

The arrangements for the disposal of sewage were primitive and curious. In some cases it was emptied into a cess-pool in the middle of the yard where it accumulated over a period of years. In other yards all refuse, including human, vegetable and animal matter, was spread over the surface of the yard and allowed to dry so that it could be sold to farmers as manure for their fields. Sometimes a cellar was used as a cess-pit and in Kirtley's Yard people lived over one such cellar, separated from it by only a wooden floor which had several holes through the boards.

The contents of the cess-pits often percolated into the water supply which came from underground springs and wells (Fordyce, 1856, 39). Apart from private or shared sources

of water within the yards, there were five public wells and a spring on the Demesnes which ran so slowly that people had to queue before they could fill their receptacles to take home. There is evidence that the churchyard was also responsible for some of the contamination of the water which ran downhill from the burial area.

Ill-health inevitably followed from these circumstances and rose to a climax in the Asiatic Cholera epidemic of 1849 when the illness proved to be most virulent in the areas of the town where the factory workers lived. The lower end of

Fig. 46. Photograph of Robert Johnson Cain (1842-1924), carpet weaver, and his wife, Eliza Wright (1849-1926), of Thorngate Wynd, Barnard Castle. They married in 1889, after the death of Robert's first wife, a spinner in the flax mill. Eliza was companion to Mrs. Badcock (a daughter of Joshua Monkhouse). Robert and his older brother, John, also a carpet weaver, were born at Castle Scar (fig. 47), sons of John Cain (1781-1851), a carpet weaver according to the 1841 census and most likely to have been employed by the Monkhouse company (being a Methodist). The 1851 census described him as a handloom woollen weaver. This kept open the option of going into other branches of the woollen trade, indicating that the carpet industry was already in decline.

Fig. 47. Photograph taken from the path which leads from the County bridge to the castle showing how all the narrow space between the river and castle was used for houses with one cottage (home of Robert Johnson Cain) perched precariously on the steep bank, its back against the curtain wall, high above Dunn's mill.

the town was most afflicted and statistics showed that those living below the Market Cross were eight times more likely to die of cholera than those living above that point (Ranger 1850, 4). It was also demonstrated that the users of particular sources of water were also more likely to be afflicted: in Swinburne's Yard (off Thorngate) fifteen of the thirty-two residents died, and other people who had shared the yard's water supply also contracted cholera; altogether forty-three people had used the water and twenty-eight of them died. A local surgeon, Mr. Cust, observed, 'I am of opinion that the water in this well is poisoned by the drainage' (Ranger, 1850, 11).

Other unhealthy aspects of the area that housed most of the factory workers were: disused tanning works in which, in one case, thirty-five pits were filled with stagnant animal and vegetable refuse; the proximity of slaughter houses and the inadequate disposal of refuse from them. The practice of keeping animals, especially pigs, in the yards, made conditions even worse. There were 377 cases of cholera in Barnard Castle and 1,297 cases of premonitory diarrhoea from 24 August to 18 October, 1849. A total of 145 died in that period (Fordyce, 1856, 38).

The degrading conditions in which the workers generally lived led to a correspondingly low standard of mental and moral outlook. Mr. William Ranger, the inspector who wrote the *Report to the General Board of Health* (1850), said that the people were 'destitute of the means of observing the ordinary rules of decency' because of their physical surroundings, including shared living and sleeping accommodation for adults and children of all ages and both sexes. In the same report, the Rev. G. Dugard, the incumbent of St. Mary's (later the parish church) reported indifference to 'religious ordinances and responsibility' (p.18) 'Their wretched homes are abodes of filth, with all the miserable concomitants of squalid poverty' (p.19). Gambling, drunkenness and sexual laxity were specifically mentioned.

Criminal behaviour is reported from other sources. Mr. Justice Cresswell, at the County Assizes on 6 March 1851 was sentencing a Barnard Castle man for assaulting a women, when he read out a list of his previous offences and commented that the man was a fair specimen of the men of Barnard Castle which he described as a 'sink of vice and profligacy'. G. Layton, in 1823, was more specific about the criminal area of the town:

> 'Next Bridgegate comes, all Barnard's muddy sink,
> where reigns, supremely great, the god of s..nk:
> Thy crimes unseemly would disgrace my lay,
> So let them sleep, nor see the light of day'.

Practices specific to the carpet industry were also blamed by Rev. Mr. Dugard, for the apprentice and the draw-boy systems resulted in girls and boys of twelve or thirteen years old receiving into their own hands, wages which were sufficient to make them independent of their parents, though not enough to give them a decent standard of living. Mr. Dugard declared that boys and girls of fifteen or sixteen 'quit the paternal roof and shamelessly co-habit together'. Mr. Ranger was given lists of names of 'parties thus living ... some with children ... from one to eight in number' (Ranger, 1850, 19).

In 1838 George Brown, who was Clerk to the Poor Law Union, compiled a report on *'The mode of living of the labourers and operatives within the district of the Teesdale Union'*. He showed that a carpet weaver was paid twice as much as a farm labourer but 'in a general way he never saves a farthing against the hour of mercantile distress, slackness of work etc., and when he is deprived of work for a week or a fortnight, his family is instantly in destitution'. Mr. Brown asserted that he and other observers agreed that 'three out of every four of these carpet weavers' spent a quarter of their income on 'articles of spirituous liquors and ale'. He added, 'They absolutely think of little but eating and drinking'. (Brown, 1837)

Mr. Brown, like the Rev. Mr. Dugard, used emotive language when writing about the carpet weavers, and it is probable that local people were somewhat unfair in their strong condemnation of the factory workers. No reference is made to the fact that the report reveals that the weavers' families were far better fed than the farm labourers', even allowing for their relative wages. The labourer spent only 6d on meat from the butcher (usually on offal) whereas the weaver spent three shillings on butcher's meat. The report gives the agricultural workers' average wage as ten shillings per week, without taking into account that his income increased during the summer months whereas the weaver, whose average wage was given as £1, sometimes received no income at all for varying periods.

Work in the carpet factories was very irregular and weavers were often unemployed for periods of three to ten days at a time. Periodic idleness led to drinking, then shortage of money and then theft. When work was available it was often very concentrated, and the shift system, especially the night shift, was debilitating. A working day of sixteen hours was particularly injurious to health and spirits when it followed a period of inadequate feeding due to unemployment. These alternate periods of intense labour and enforced idleness were caused by factory owners who took orders which could not be completed by an agreed date unless men worked throughout the night. This might be followed by a period in which no further orders were received. Two weavers, H. MacKay and W. Baker, deplored this system and added that in districts where long hours and night work had been given up, great benefits had been felt by both the employer and the employed (Ranger, 1850, 20-21).

Another fault in the carpet industry was that apprenticeships lasted for far too long and it was not unknown for a 'life apprenticeship' to be arranged. One, at least, of the factory owners, Messrs. Monkhouse and Sons, deplored this practice. Mr. Monkhouse took boys at the age of fourteen. For the first three years the boy allowed his master 25 per cent of his earnings (say eight shillings per week) and then for the remaining four years the master took twelve shillings per week. The employee ended his apprenticeship at the age of twenty-one. Some other employers were not so generous, and extracted payments from their apprentices in other ways. Others took on apprentices at too young an age, and all of them (even the better employers) made the apprenticeship last too long, if J. Baker, one of the carpet weavers, was correct, for he asserted that 'every description of carpet-weaving is easily learnt in a period of three years' (Ranger, 1850, 21).

It was difficult for the weavers to obtain any help in such matters, but various official and benevolent bodies offered to help when sufferings were caused by poverty and ill-health. In recognition of the weavers' intermittent periods of unem-

ployment, the Overseers of the Poor could make discretionary awards to 'the weavers and families out of employ' (Vestry Minutes) and, if the worst happened, there was the Poor House (in Thorngate) and later the Workhouse (in Galgate). The former was the more kindly disposed and its provisions for weavers in particular included three weaving looms and a warping mill for those who were 'able' (fig. 48). There was also a Sunday school for children who worked in local factories. In 1762 there were twenty inmates of the Poor House, a figure which rose to sixty-five in 1834 -

Fig. 48. A female worker 'drawing in' worsted warp, illustrated in *The Pictorial Gallery of Arts*, Charles Knight, 1858-60.

though it must not be assumed that the carpet industry was solely responsible for this increase; there were other factors such as the Enclosure Acts.

There were also benevolent organizations, such as three clothing societies, a charity for poor women in child-birth (Fordyce, 1856, 42), and the Barnard Castle Dispensary for the Relief of the Sick Poor. It was founded in 1835 with 175 patients, rising to 216 in 1841, 'during the great depression in town and district'. In 1876 there were 275 patients 'chiefly owing to the closure of Thorngate Mill leading to poverty

and low diet'. In 1885, as the carpet industry declined, there were 300 patients. (Dispensary Minutes, as recorded in the *Teesdale Mercury* 11 March 1891 & subsequent issues)

The Local Board of Health (established in 1850 as a result of William Ranger's report) tried to help in a more general way. The Board immediately set about creating a water supply from a specially constructed reservoir, and also laid a fairly comprehensive network of sewers though there was no

Fig. 49. Postcard, c.1894, looking westward along Bridgegate. The general air of dilapidation is evident and it is easy to see why the planners of the 1930s and 1950s decided on a programme of rebuilding.

sewage works until 1875. However, the poorest area in which the carpet weavers and other factory hands worked benefited least. Their dwellings were too densely packed together for proper underground sewers to be laid, so earth and pail closets were still widely used, and the water supply was often limited to a shared tap in a yard. There was no demolition of unfit dwellings, and no method was found to create currents of air to flow through the damp yards; no *cul de sac* became a thoroughfare. Tenants were encouraged to limewash their premises to make them brighter and cleaner, but in some cases this was little more than a cosmetic treatment. The inhabitants were slow to improve their habitual standards, though eventually their shortcomings were recognised as being to a large extent the result of their social context.

In general, the rest of the town improved more rapidly and effectively. The Market Place was made cleaner and tidier; the cattle market was moved from Galgate to purpose-built premises on the north-western edge of town; trees, grass plots, flower beds and an ornamental drinking fountain improved the appearance of Galgate; trees were planted in Newgate (and also in Thorngate) and some new and quite dignified houses rose in the upper part of the town.

As the carpet industry declined, Barnard Castle maintained its ancient role of market town and began also to emerge as an attractive tourist centre. Though the concealed yards and the street of Bridgegate remained largely unchanged (fig. 49), the appearance of the rest of the town received many favourable comments.

On 18 March 1891 an editorial in the *Teesdale Mercury* included this observation: '... one cannot help feeling a tinge of sadness in reflecting on a decayed industry. But, after all, the Barnard Castle of today is, I am sure, to be preferred to what it was in those days when the busy hum of the mill was in full swing, and when the town was trusting to its soon-to-decay industries instead of, as now, striving by sanitary and progressive measures of many sorts to make Barnard Castle one of the favourite sanitoriums of the north of England'.

Fig. 50. Photograph of the County bridge and its surroundings. In the fore-ground is the weir which directed
water to the factories at the foot of Thorngate. It also
shows the crush of buildings between river and castle.
The tallest building is Dunn's Factory.

CHAPTER 9

THEN AND NOW: VISIBLE EVIDENCE

Most of the houses in which the carpet weavers lived were demolished in the 1930s and 1950s in successive schemes for rehousing people who were living in conditions which were considered unsuitable and could not reasonably be made habitable. It was a long and, in some cases, controversial process; modern conservationists would have saved more of the eighteenth-century houses, perhaps, but much of the demolition was seen at the time as inevitable and necessary. A wider road bordered by grassy slopes and trees was created in Bridgegate, opening up views of the castle and river that had not been seen for perhaps five hundred years. The grass and trees cover the rubble of former houses and factories, but some traces of these buildings can still be seen. Parts of the

Fig. 51. Photograph of the site of Dunn's carpet factory, 1996, a comparison with fig. 37 and fig. 50.

cliff on which the castle stands are indented with rectangular sockets for joists and beams of houses which used the rock face as their back wall, and one or two patches of limewash can also be seen, presumably put there at the suggestion of the first Local Board of Health for Barnard Castle on what was then an internal wall. Two houses in Bridgegate have survived from the days of the carpet factories. One is a public house, The Oddfellows' Arms, and the other is an eighteenth-century three-storey dwelling attached to the former carpet factory extending to the river. This was Raine's factory and it bears a carved stone dated 1839. The building is now in commercial use as a tyre depot and the house has been restored to domestic use by owners who take a great interest in its history (figs 30-33). The factory itself has a former loading bay facing onto the river; the door is about four feet above the average level of the water nowadays (plate 14), but when there was a weir at the end of Thorngate Wynd the water was higher (fig. 50). The loading door shows that the river was used by boats which conveyed materials to and from the dye-pits farther along the river bank.

The dye-pits in the river frontage of what was once Dunn's carpet factory (fig. 38) are now covered by a sloping grass plot with self-sown young ash trees growing on it (fig. 51). This was the last of the vanished factories to be demolished; it was about 150 yards upstream of Raine's factory. The lower stone courses of the riverside factories that have been demolished now form the retaining wall that runs along the stretch of river between the County Bridge and the end of Thorngate Wynd, where the remains of the weir can still be seen. There are large smooth blocks of stone which formed the sloping downstream side of the weir, several of them still in place; large oak beams were bolted to its upstream side and one of these is visible in the water beside the weir. The weir deflected water to drive the machinery of Thorngate Mill, built in 1847-8 as a spinning mill for Messrs. Monkhouse, which stands immediately upstream of the Thorngate footbridge (fig. 52). This became a woollen mill which later made tweed 'pieces'. Traces of the sluice-gatehouse and the groove that held the sluice-gate in a vertical position can be seen near the weir, and the entrance and exit of the millrace are still visible at the foot of the gable ends of the mill itself.

In Thorngate, another building of Monkhouse's carpet factory still stands, with a stone in the wall dating the building to 1846 (fig. 35). The factory is now divided into dwellings and the old entry for wagons has been filled in.

On the opposite (west) side of the street are seventeenth and eighteenth-century weavers' houses, recognisable by the con-

tinuous rows of windows in the top storeys. The windows are separated only by stone mullions so that as much light as possible could fall on the looms. Two such houses have been preserved as modern dwellings by the Teesdale Buildings Preservation Trust (fig. 3). Weavers' windows can also be seen in The White Swan, at Bridge End, just over the County bridge (fig. 53).

In Thorngate, The Bank, the Market Place and the Horse Market there are still entrances to yards which once contained the insalubrious houses of industrial workers. Some of these yards are private but others are pedestrian thoroughfares. Those on The Bank lead to the Demesnes, an area of grass land, where the workers went to collect water from the spring or to walk freely in the open countryside. Waterloo Yard, on the east side of the Market Place, leads to the old Back Lane on the east of the town. Others still lead to houses in *culs de sac*, but the houses are of more recent date or have been converted into conformity with modern standards. In these cases more light and air have been introduced over the years by the judicious demolition of old buildings, and the result is a sequestered residential area of some charm. As in days of old, a casual passer-by would have no idea of the housing that lies behind the frontages of the main street (fig. 54).

Several shops in the town sold carpets in the nineteenth century. Some of these shops have survived but, like the existing factories, have changed their function. The shop of J. Howson was called Teesdale House when it sold carpets in the 1870s at the junction of Hall Street and the Market Place; it now sells

Fig. 52. Thorngate Mill photographed in 1996, in use as a wholesale book warehouse. The first footbridge on the site built in 1871 was swept away in the flood of 1881. (See also figs 5 and 25)

Fig. 53. The County Bridge and the White Swan Inn at the south end. Note the 'weavers windows' under the eaves. This seems to have been the building flooded in 1771 with unexpected benefits to the dyer who occupied it (Chapter 1).

car accessories. John Parkinson's premises from which carpets were sold in the 1880s in Horse Market now form part of Boyes' department store. Commerce House, from which J. Garbutt sold carpets (advertising 1867-85) on The Bank has been demolished and replaced (in 1987) by a modern building in the eighteenth century style. The address of the shop belonging to J. M. Marshall, carpet salesman (from 1867), was not mentioned on his advertisement but his name survives in Marshall Street, leading off the north side of Galgate.

The names of some of the factory owners themselves survive over their graves in the old churchyard or the 'new' cemetery, consecrated in 1865, off Victoria Road. Some of the headstones or table tombs are inscribed with the professions as well as the names of the men whom they commemorate.

Fig. 54. Priory Yard, watercolour by Lucy Errington, about 1967. The cholera epidemic was most virulent here, according to the *Report of the General Board of Health,* The yard had 15 tenements occupied by 64 persons with one privy to 15 houses and a very large cesspool in the centre (Ranger, 1850, p.13 and 18).

In the churchyard there is a cluster of graves of the Monkhouse family, just across the little path at the north-east corner of the parish church. One of them records 'Ebenezer Monkhouse, formerly of Barnard Castle, carpet manufacturer' (He died in Stewiacke, Nova Scotia in 1863, aged 65).

Thomas Dixon, manufacturer, who died in 1826, aged seventy-four, lies a few yards to the west of the sloping path that runs through the old churchyard from Newgate to the Demesnes. On the south side of the churchyard there is a memorial in the form of a cross on a chamfered plinth which commemorates the victims of the cholera epidemic in 1849 (fig. 55). Nearby, on the opposite side of the path, is the grave of John Pratt (fig. 56) who owned one of the biggest carpet factories and who died of the same illness in the same epidemic, at the age of forty-six.

In the Victoria Road cemetery are the graves of Joshua Monkhouse, (1782-1866), carpet manufacturer, and several of his relatives; these graves are close to the path just south-east of the chapel. In the south east corner of the Non-conformist cemetery is an obelisk commemorating Edward Raine (1786-1867), a prominent Presbyterian, and also a carpet manufacturer.

The relics of the carpet factories, whether by the river, in the streets, or in the burial grounds of Barnard Castle, are silent reminders of the time when 'the busy hum of the mill' was an important feature in the life of the town.

Fig. 55. Memorial to the victims of the cholera epedemic, 1849. The inscription reads: *In memory of the inhabitants of Barnard Castle, who died of Asiatic Cholera from August 18th to October 1849. In the midst of life we are in death.*

Fig. 56. Gravestone of John Pratt. The inscription reads:
JOHN PRATT
who departed this life September 2nd 1849
aged 46 years
Also Catherine daughter of the above
who died Sep 2nd 1849 aged 11 years
And of Sarah Ann who died
Aug 29th 1849 aged 3 years
Also Margaret and Mary Jane, who
died in their infancy.
Also Thomas PATTISON PRATT son
of the above who died 18th August 1856
aged 17 year.

CATALOGUE OF CARPETS

This is a catalogue of carpets shown in the exhibition held at The Bowes Museum, 21 September 1996 to 5 January 1997. Many of the entries include dye and fibre analyses by Dr. Taylor and Dr. Ryder. A grant from the Pasold Research Fund helped towards this work, but it is not complete owing to lack of time and further resources. However, it does provide a starting point for further research and comparative studies of carpets from other areas. The Textile Department of the University of Huddersfield have generously assisted with further technical analysis. Two M.Sc students have provided the count and twist tests on the yarns and analysed the carpet tapes. Their full technical analysis of each carpet cannot be included here, but it has enabled them to reproduce samples for the exhibition based on the point paper designs. The re-creation of these textiles on a Jacquard hand-loom will increase our understanding of how these carpets were originally made. All the carpets (except nos. 11 and 13) would have been woven on a 36 inch wide loom, even though the actual finished width recorded below tends to vary between 33 and 36 inches owing to the finishing processes and shrinkage.

1. Three pieces of flat-woven carpeting, Kidderminster type (plate 3)

Barnard Castle, Co. Durham, 19th century, second quarter
Plain weave double cloth, wool, worsted warps, woollen wefts, with goat hair present in one yarn
Woven in a small diaper pattern forming diamonds enclosing a lobed motif, in pink, greens, brown, black and natural, some edges bound with striped woollen braid
Pattern repeat: $2^{3}/8$ in x $2^{1}/8$ in (6 x 5.5 cm)
Finished width: $34^{1}/2$ in (87.5 cm)
Overall sizes: A = $19^{1}/2$ in x $12^{1}/2$ in (49.5 x 32 cm), B = 35in x 19in (89 x 48.5 cm), C = 11ft 9in x 4ft $10^{1}/2$ in (358 x 148.5 cm) made up of one full width plus a $22^{1}/2$ in (57 cm) strip sewn together.

Provenance: Given to The Bowes Museum by Miss Lucy Errington and her brother at different dates (1936, 1944 and 1958). She stated that the carpet had been made from the wool of sheep on her grandmother's farm, Stoney Keld, Bowes, in Teesdale. The wool, said to have been plucked from the sheep's back (note plucked, not shorn), was spun in the farmhouse and woven at a Barnard Castle carpet factory especially for the family. There were about one hundred yards of the carpet origi-nally. Another piece is still in private ownership, inherited from a different line of the family.

Literature: C. Gilbert, J. Lomax, A. Wells-Cole, *Country House Floors 1660-1850*, Temple Newsam House Studies, No. 3. (Leeds City Art Galleries, 1987) cat. no. 63, p. 92, plate 12c (henceforth *Country House Floors*)

Exhibitions: as above, Temple Newsam, Leeds, 1987

This simple diaper pattern was a very traditional design common in the 18th century. A painting of about 1770, English School, shows a similar carpet in use (Leeds City Art Galleries, illus. in *Country House Floors* No. 64). The design is close to a piece of English or Scottish carpeting in Boston, dated 1770 to 1810 (Kraak, 1996, p. 188 plate XIV). This carpet has been compared to one in the Colonial Williamsburg Foundation (discussed below, cat. no. 2) Before the Jacquard mechanism was employed, only these small-scale geometric patterns could be produced on a draw-loom.

The Bowes Museum, accession nos. 1936.35, 1944.17, 1961.86 (Carpet 15 a,b,c)

Technical Details: Ends per inch = 32, Picks per inch = 28

Colour	Dye analysis by Dr. Taylor	Yarn Thickness	Yarn Construction	Fibre analysis/fleece type by Dr. Ryder
natural	not tested [undyed]	warp, thin	2 ply singles, Z, S-spun	wool, blend of hairy + medium hairy
green	Saxe blue + trace mordant yellow ?	warp, thin	2 ply singles, Z, S-spun	wool, either hairy type or blend of hairy and medium hairy
red/brown	not identified unknown dyewood?	warp, thin	2 ply singles, Z, S-spun	wool, blend of hairy and medium
natural	not tested [undyed]	weft, thick	single, Z spun	wool, hairy and medium
pink/red	cochineal	weft, thick	single, Z-spun	wool, hairy type or blend of hairy and medium hairy
brown	tannin	weft, thick	single, Z-spun	wool, blended hairy and medium hairy
black	tannin	weft, thick	single, Z-spun	wool, blended hairy and medium hairy
green	Saxe blue + trace mordant yellow?	weft, thick	single, Z-spun	wool, blended hairy medium hairy
olive green	Saxe blue + trace mordant yellow?	weft, thick	single, Z-spun	wool, hairy fleece type, some goat hairs

2. Piece of flat-woven carpeting, Kidderminster type (plate 4)

English, place of manufacture unknown, late 18th century/early 19th century

Plain weave double cloth, worsted wool warps, woollen wefts

Small diaper pattern with octagons and squares in green, pink, browns, natural

Pattern repeat: 2 x 2¼ in (5 x 5.5 cm) Approx.

Finished width: 36 in (91cm)

Provenance: Gift of Mrs. John D. Rockefeller III, New York, to Colonial Williamsburg Foundation

Literature: Mildred B. Lanier, *English and Oriental Carpets at Williamsburg,* (Charlottesville, 1975), no. 12

It was not possible to include this carpet in the exhibition, but in 1990 it was compared, side by side with cat. no. 1. Not only did the range of colours appear to be the same, but they were combined together in the same order to create the coloured banding in the weft. The three colours used in the warp are the same in both carpets. The yarn and dye analysis offers a more detailed comparison and reveals that the fleece types, yarn thickness and construction are very similar. As was to be expected, the same range of natural dyes has been identified. However, it is not possible, within the scope of this study, to draw further conclusions as to the place of manufacture within England.

Colonial Williamsburg Foundation Accession no. G.1956.297 (photograph only exhibited)

Colour	Dye analysis by Dr. Taylor	Yarn Thickness	Yarn Construction	Fibre analysis/fleece type by Dr. Ryder
natural	not tested [undyed]	warp, thin	2 ply, singles, S-spun	wool, blend of hairy or medium hairy
green*	poss. Saxe blue and unidentified yellow	warp, thin	-	wool, either hairy or blend of hairy and medium hairy
red/brown	soluble redwood	warp, thin	2 ply, singles, S-spun	hairy fleece type
pink/red	not tested, [probably cochineal]	weft, thick	single,	hairy type of fleece loosely Z-spun
natural	not tested [undyed]	weft, thick	single Z-spun	hairy type of fleece
brown	tannin	weft, thick	single Z-spun	hairy type of fleece

* other green fibres in the sample were identified as Saxe blue & poss. old fustic & tannin and Saxe blue & tannin.

3. Three lengths of flat woven carpet, Kidderminster type (plate 5)

Barnard Castle, Co. Durham, about 1860

Plain weave double cloth, wool, worsted warps, woollen wefts with possibly goat hair present in one yarn

Woven in geometric grid pattern with formalised rosettes, stylised bosses and geometric motifs in red, brown, black, green and natural

Pattern repeat: 4⅝ in x 4½ in (11.9 x 10.7 cm)

Finished width: 33in (84 cm)

Overall sizes: A = 12ft 4 in x 33¾ in (376 x 86 cm), B = 12ft 2in x 33¾ in (371 x 86 cm), C = 12ft 8in x 33¾ in (385 x 86 cm)

Provenance: Purchased locally from Miss Lambert (date unknown) by The Bowes Museum

Literature: *Country House Floors,* cat. no. 62, p. 92, plate 12B

Exhibitions: Temple Newsam, Leeds, 1987

The finding of a synthetic, or chemical, dye, has provided a later date than expected. The geometric design suggests a date of 1825-50 and would have been viewed as old fashioned in the 1860s, when patterns were beginning to be more expansive. Barnard Castle manufacturers went on producing such designs probably because they were popular with a rather conservative market. There was a practical reason too, as small repeating patterns were much less wasteful when joining widths. The red banding across the pattern, formed by the weft, is at random intervals replaced by a different red. This irregular feature of an otherwise symmetrical design would have been quite obvious when the carpet was laid and was probably not intentional, but a mistake by the weaver. It perhaps suggests that these particular pieces may have been remnants or 'seconds' available only to the local population.

It is notable that this example, and cat nos. 1 and 2, have the same three colours in the warp. A three colour warp was probably standard in the production of this type of carpeting. The looms would be warped up with extremely long warps on which a variety of different patterns might be woven, the design and the colourways provided by the weft threads, which usually display a greater range of colours. This premise is borne out in Jacob Allison's accounts, which show payments to a warper only occasionally, once every two or three months.

The Bowes Museum, accession no. Carpet 1.1

Technical details: Ends per inch = 30, Picks per inch = 26

Colour	Dye analysis by Dr. Taylor	Yarn Thickness	Yarn Construction	Fibre analysis/fleece type by Dr. Ryder
natural	not tested [undyed]	warp, thick	2 ply, singles Z, S-spun	-
green	Saxe blue and mordant yellow?	warp, thick yellow	2 ply singles Z, S-spun	wool, blend of hairy and hairy medium
brown	tannin and luteolin	warp, thick	2 ply, singles Z, S-spun	wool, hairy medium
red	synthetic acid dye	weft, thin	single, Z-spun	"rough" woollen yarn of hairy fleece type
tan	tannin	weft, thin	single, Z-spun	wool, hairy fleece type
green	Saxe blue and mordant yellow?	weft, thin	single, Z-spun	-
black	logwood	weft, thin	single, Z-spun	-
natural	not tested [undyed]	weft, thin	single, Z-spun	-
red	synthetic acid dye	weft, thin	single, Z-spun	wool and hair, possibly goat (analysis by Hudd. Univ.)

4. Piece of flat-woven carpeting, Kidderminster type

Troutbeck, Cumbria, possibly 1768
Plain-weave double cloth, wool, worsted warps, woollen wefts
Woven on a square grid design containing crosses and stepped lozenges in reds, yellow, black and white

Pattern repeat:	height 6⅛ in (15.5 cm)
Finished width:	35in (89 cm)
Overall size:	60in x 35in (152 x 89 cm)

Provenance: Found in the attic at Townend, Troutbeck, together with a large carpet (9ft4in x 10ft), two door mats, two window pelmets and several pelmets - all of the same fabric. An old document attached to the carpet stated that it was 'woven in 1768 by William Birkett for the Browne family of Townend'.

Literature: *Country House Floors,* cat no. 61, p. 92, plate 13a, Hefford, 1987, 4, fig. 5a & b, Kraak, 1996, 187- 8, Plate X

Exhibitions: Temple Newsam, Leeds, 1987

Lent by The National Trust (Townend)

5. Piece of flat-woven Scotch carpeting, (plate 6)

Selkirk, Scotland, 19th century, second quarter
Plain weave, double cloth, wool, worsted warps, woollen wefts
Woven with an elaborate lattice pattern forming a compartmental design with a leaf motif in greens, red, brown, black, maroon, blue, pale pink, neutral. One edge has a striped woollen braid

Pattern repeat:	5in x 4¼ in (12.7 x 10.8 cm).
Finished width:	not known
Overall size:	4ft 6 in x 20½ in (136 x 52 cm)

Provenance: Purchased by owner at auction in Selkirk
A refined, modern reproduction has been produced from this design. A Scotch carpet from Dalkeith Palace, Lothian, Scotland (National Museums of Scotland) has a similar pattern (*Country House Floors,* no. 53)

Lent by John Claridge, Claridge Associates, Selkirk.

Technical Details:	Ends per inch = 32 Picks per inch = 28
Warp coloration:	lime green, red, brown, natural (undyed)
yarn construction:	2 ply singles Z, S spun (thin)
Weft coloration:	red, black, light green, green, natural (undyed) brown, burgundy, blue, pink.
yarn construction:	single, Z spun (thick)

6. Fragment of flat-woven carpeting, Kidderminster type (plate 11)

Probably Barnard Castle, Co. Durham, 1830-50
Plain weave double cloth, wool, worsted warps, woollen wefts
Woven design of four, five-fingered leaves within a square, forming central four-petalled flower shape in red and natural, with black introduced as a band through the flower centre.

Pattern repeat:	unknown. Square leaf design: 13in x 12¾in (33 x 32 cm)
Finished width:	unknown
Overall size:	19¾ in x 13½in (50 x 34 cm)

Provenance; Found in a dolls' house. The house, about 1830, was given to The Bowes Museum in 1940 by Mrs. Frank Bell, Stubb House, Barnard Castle

The Bowes Museum accession no. 1940.20 (Toy.311)

The dolls' house is in the form of a cabinet, like a 17th century dolls' house, but made, probably locally, in a very simple fashion. It is quite likely that this scrap of carpeting was made in Barnard Castle.

The pleasing simplicity of this design (or part design) using bold natural forms within a square block is reminiscent of North Country quilt designs. It also compares with the carpet designs by Pratt, Son & Co., registered in 1842 (figs 18-19).

Technical details:	Ends per inch = 24 Picks per inch = 24
warp coloration:	red, natural (undyed)
yarn construction:	2 ply singles, S spun (thick)
weft coloration:	orange, red, black, undyed
yarn construction:	2 ply singles, S spun (thick)

7. Carpet made from three strips of flat-woven carpeting, Kidderminster type (plate 8)

Barnard Castle, Co. Durham, 1840-60
Plain weave double cloth, wool, worsted warps, woollen wefts.
Woven with a large repeating medallion, a double motif to each width. On the face which has been uppermost, the design, in yellow ochre, is seen against bands of changing colours in the weft. The colours are an unusual combination of pinks and yellows, with darker bands of brown and black. There are three colours in the warp (like cat no. 1, 2 and 3) but six in the weft. The three widths are hand-stitched together, joined without a drop in the repeat. One of the cut edges is bound under with a striped woollen tape.

Pattern repeat:	20³/4 in x 16³/4 in (53 x 42.5 cm)
Finished width:	33³/4 in (85.7 cm)
Overall size:	12ft 2¹/2 in x 8ft 4¹/2 in (371 x 254 cm)

Provenance: From Mount Eff Cottage, Westwick, Barnard Castle, where it was used as an underlay for another carpet for about twenty years. The owners, Mr. & Mrs. J. Pounder donated it to The Bowes Museum in 1990. It is thought that it may have been used at Abbey Farm, Egglestone Abbey, Barnard Castle, or bought in the local sale-room.

Exhibitions: *Restored to View*, The Bowes Museum, 1991, featuring the conservation treatment of the carpet

This complete carpet illustrates well the 'stripy' effect which was so characteristic of Kidderminster carpeting and shows the effectiveness of the more ambitious repeating design. This large, curvilinear design would have been woven on a loom with a Jacquard attachment. The design is similar to a number of American examples, particularly one in Winterthur Museum, English or American, 1830-50 (Kraak, 1996, p. 186, plate. VII)

The Bowes Museum, accession no. 1990.7 (Carpet 3.1)

Technical details: Ends per inch = 32, Picks per inch = 28

Colour	Dye analysis by Dr. Taylor	Yarn Thickness	Yarn Construction	Fibre analysis/fleece type by Dr. Ryder
*ochre	probably quercetin	warp, thin	2 ply singles Z, S-spun	wool, hairy medium
*pink	probably soluble redwood	warp, thin	2 ply singles, Z, S-spun	wool, hair medium
*light pink	probably soluble redwood	warp, thin	2 ply singles, Z, S spun	-
ochre	quercetin	weft, thick	Single, S-spun	wool, hairy medium
pink	soluble redwood	weft thick	Single, S-spun	-
light pink	probably soluble redwood	weft, thick	Single, S-spun	-
red/brown	tannin + luteolin	weft, thick	Single, S-spun	wool, hairy medium
grey/black	probably logwood	weft, thick	Single, S-spun	-
*yellow	quercetin?	weft, thick	Single, S-spun	-

* not tested

8. Two pieces of flat-woven carpeting, Kidderminster type (plate 9)

Barnard Castle, Co, Durham, 1840-60
Plain weave, triple cloth, wool, worsted warps, woollen wefts
Woven in an imitation Turkish carpet design, two alternating medallions, one eight pointed enclosing a cross shape, the other a quatrefoil shape, in red, green and buff

Pattern repeat: 40³/4 in x 33 in (103.5 x 84 cm)
Finished width: 33in (84 cm)
Overall size: 9ft x 2ft 9in (274 x 84 cm)
                    plus small fragment 9in x 33in (23 x 84 cm)

Provenance: Found uncatalogued in 1972 with an old label attached inscribed 'piece of Barnard Castle carpet c. 1850'. Thought to be the carpeting given in June 1964 by Mrs. Simpson, Brignall, Barnard Castle.

Literature: S.B. Sherrill *Carpets & Rugs of Europe & America,* Abbeville Press, 1996, p.215-6, plate 240

It is most likely that this example was made in Barnard Castle. There is, as yet, no other evidence for triple cloth being made in the town, but most manufacturers of double cloth could and probably did make triple cloth as the same looms could produce both types. Both 3-ply and 2-ply were classed as Kidderminsters, sometimes 3-ply was called 'Imperial Kidderminster'. Perhaps in Barnard Castle the 'Super Kidder' produced by Jacob Allison was in fact 3-ply.

Turkey-pattern designs were widely used in printed floor cloths of this period. A floor cloth with a similar design to this carpet, dated 1847, is illustrated in *Country House Floors* (cat. 75).

The Bowes Museum, accession no. 1964.515 (carpet 2.8)

Technical details: Ends per inch = 48, Picks per inch = 36

Colour	Dye analysis by Dr. Taylor	Yarn Thickness	Yarn Construction	Fibre analysis/fleece type by Dr. Ryder
*red	prob. cochineal	warp, thin, S-spun	2 ply, singles, Z	wool, hairy
*green	prob. tannin with iron mordant	warp, thin,	2 ply, singles Z, S-spun	wool, hairy
*buff	prob. undyed	warp, thin,	single, S-spun	wool, hairy medium
red	cochineal	weft, thick,	single, S-spun	wool, hairy medium
green	tannin with iron mordant	weft, thick	single, S-spun	wool, hairy medium
light green	tannin with iron mordant	weft, thick,	single, S-spun	wool, hairy medium

* not tested

9. Piece of flat-woven carpet, Kidderminster type (fig. 12)

British, place of manufacture unknown, 1830-40
Plain weave, triple cloth, wool, worsted warps, woollen wefts
Woven in a large-scale elaborate pattern with large rosettes and stars surrounded by acanthus fronds within a linear pavement design, in three colours, red-brown, light tan and cream

Pattern repeat: 75in x 35in (190 x 89 cm)
Finished width: 35in (89 cm)
Overall size: 3ft   2¹/4 in x 35in (97 x 89 cm)

Provenance: Part of a fitted carpet in the Long Gallery at Burton Constable near Hull, shown in a coloured lithograph of 1836-9 (plate 2)

Literature: *Country House Floors,* cat no. 51, p. 72

Exhibitions: Temple Newsam, Leeds, 1987

The bill, for what would have been a large amount of carpeting (the Long Gallery is over 100 feet long) has not come to light. Other bills for carpeting Burton Constable which have survived show that they used a local supplier Fearne & Eastern, 8 Market Place, Hull, 'Dealers in Brussels, Kidderminster, Scotch and Venetian Carpets'. Bills from them in 1837, and during the 1840's, included the purchase of '1 large hearth rug to match Leopard carpet' and Brussels carpeting. Also in the 1840's, Alfred Lapworth & Co., Carpet Manufacturers, supplied carpet to Burton Constable. They were one of the firms Jacob Allison supplied in the 1830's. Barnard Castle goods could have been supplied to Hull, a major coastal port & served by Stocton-on-Tees.

Lent by John Chichester-Constable

Technical Details   Ends per inch = 45, Picks per inch = 45

Colour	Dye analysis not undertaken	Yarn Thickness	Yarn Construction	Fibre analysis/fleece type by Dr. Ryder
light tan	-	warp, thin	?	-
red-brown	-	warp, thin	?	-
cream	prob. undyed	warp, thin	?	wool, hairy medium
light tan	-	weft, thick	single, S-spun	wool, hairy medium
red-brown	-	weft, thick	single, Z-spun	wool, blend of hairy and hairy medium
cream	prob. undyed	weft, thick	single, Z-spun	wool, hairy medium

10. Length of flat-woven carpeting, Kidderminster type

British, place of manufacture not known, 1840-50
Plain weave, triple cloth, wool, worsted warps, woollen wefts
Woven in a large ambitious design based on architectural motifs in a mirrored repeat within a larger medallion

Pattern repeat: 7ft 8in x 35 in (233.5 x 89 cm)
Finished loom width: 35in (89 cm)
Overall size: 8ft 8in x 5ft 10 in (263 x 176.5 cm)

Provenance: Unknown

If this grand design can be traced in the design registers, the identity of the very confident manufacturer will be revealed. The enormous scale of the design would need a large interior. Perhaps Monkhouse had seen something similar before they registered their design in 1845 which also includes minarets and other architectural features (plate 12)

Lent by Miss W. Hefford

Technical Details:
warp colouration: red, brown, yellow, blue, white
yarn thickness: thin
yarn construction: 2 ply, singles, Z, S-spun
weft coloration: brown, red, blue, white, yellow
yarn thickness: brown and blue thick, red, white and yellow thin
yarn construction: brown, red = single, S-spun, blue, white, yellow = single, Z-spun

11. Length of flat-woven Venetian carpeting (plate 7)

Possibly Monkhouse, Barnard Castle, Co. Durham, about 1860
Warp-faced, twill weave, single cloth, known as Venetian, wool, worsted warps, thick black wool weft
Woven in elaborate, multi-coloured stripes forming diagonal and chevron patterns within the stripes, each made up of many shades, making a total of 17 colours in the weft

Pattern repeat: 2 3/4 in x 11 in (7 x 28 cm) mirror repeat
Finished loom width: 22in (59 cm)
Overall size: 19ft 2 in x 21 3/4 in (584 x 55 cm)

Provenance: Raby Castle, County Durham. Used on back stairways and corridors; some matching pieces are still in place in a bedroom passage in Clifford's Tower. A piece of this carpet is in the collection of Leeds City Art Galleries

Literature: *Country House Floors*, cat. no. 65, p. 94, plate 14a

Exhibitions: Temple Newsam, Leeds, 1987

Dye analysis has shown that this Venetian must date from after 1860 as it contains synthetic dyes. It is not therefore the '5/8 Venetian' listed in a bill of 1845 from Joshua Monkhouse and Sons. This later version, perhaps a replacement for that bought in 1845, may still have been supplied by Monkhouse, but before 1863, as that is the year they closed down. Huddersfield University has pointed out that this example has a very complex construction and coloration plan and to weave this carpet would have been costly. This may indicate that the design was specially commissioned for Raby Castle, though the earlier Monkhouse bills do not reveal any special orders. A matching woollen tape binds the cut ends.

Lent by Lord Barnard, Raby Castle

Technical Details: Ends per inch = 76 (some ends working together in 2's and 3's) Picks per inch = 36 (3 ends working together)

Colour	Dye analysis by Dr. Taylor	Yarn Thickness	Yarn Construction	Fibre analysis/fleece type by Dr. Ryder
yellow	synthetic acid dye	warp, thin	3 ply, singles, Z S-spun	-
dark green	Saxe blue + probable luteolin	warp, thin	3 ply, singles, Z S-spun	-
bright red	synthetic acid dye	warp, thin	3 ply, singles, Z S-spun	-
maroon	synthetic acid dye	warp, thin	3 ply, singles. Z, S-spun	-
orange	synthetic acid dye	warp, thin	3 ply, singles, Z, S-spun	-
pink	synthetic acid dye	warp, thin	3 ply, singles, Z S-spun	wool, medium
natural	prob. undyed	warp, thin	3 ply, singles, Z S-spun	wool, medium hairy
pinky/beige	-	warp, thin	3 ply, singles, Z, S-spun	wool, medium hairy
light brown	-	warp, thin	3 ply, singles, Z, S-spun	wool, hairy medium
red	-	warp, thin	3 ply, singles, Z, S-spun	-
dark red	-	warp, thin	3 ply, singles, Z, S-spun	-
dark olive	-	warp, thin	3 ply, singles, Z, S-spun	-
mid olive	-	warp, thin	3 ply, singles, Z, S-spun	-
light olive	-	warp, thin	3 ply, singles, Z, S-spun	-
black	-	warp, thin	3 ply, singles, Z, S-spun	-
black	tannin	weft, v thick	3 ply, singles S-spun	wool, hairy type contains goat hairs

12. Length of flat-woven carpeting, Figured Venetian type (fig. 10)

Possibly Joshua Monkhouse & Sons, Barnard Castle, Co. Durham, 1845-9
Warp-faced, twill-weave, single cloth, wool, worsted warps, woollen wefts
Woven in a small diamond design known as a 'birds-eye' pattern, in three colours, brown, red-brown and light tan

Pattern repeat: 2 1/2 in x 1 3/4 in (6.4 x 4.4 cm)
Finished width: 35 1/2 in (90.2 cm)
Overall size: 13ft 7 1/2 in x 3 ft (415 x 91.5 cm)

Provenance: Part of a fitted carpet which is still in place in a small bedroom in Clifford's Tower, Raby Castle. The bedroom next door also has the same carpet. This example may be one of the many purchases made of 'sup. Fig'd Venetian' by Raby, itemised in bills of 1845 and 1849, from Joshua Monkhouse and Sons (fig.9).

It is reversible, like Kidderminster, though not a double cloth but woven in a warp twill like the striped Venetian (cat. no.11) so that the weft (a very thick black woollen yarn) is completely hidden. The pattern helps to confirm Wendy Hefford's suggestion that a warp-faced 'birds-eye' pattern carpet in the Victoria & Albert Museum (T.216.1976) might be a figured Venetian (Hefford 1986, p. 5, fig. 8). This piece has both wool and linen wefts, which accords with the definition in Ure's *Dictionary* (1878) whereas in the Raby example the weft is all wool. This carpet has been subjected to more wear than the striped Venetian and has faded to a green colour owing to the dyes used (see Appendix 2) which are all natural. It is very probable that it dates from the 1840s, when major refurbishing of Raby Castle was being carried out.

There is little evidence for the practice of turning these reversible types, presumably because once a carpet was fitted it would have been a major task to lift it for turning. As most rooms are not symmetrical, re-fitting would also be necessary. (The carpets in The Bowes Museum also show significant wear on one side only).

Lent by Lord Barnard, Raby Castle

Technical details: Ends per inch = 18 (2 threads working as 1), Picks per inch = 12

Colour	Dye analysis by Dr. Taylor	Yarn Thickness	Yarn Construction	Fibre analysis/fleece type by Dr. Ryder
brown	soluble redwood	warp, thin	2 ply, singles, Z, S-spun	wool, hairy medium
red-brown	lichen purple + luteolin	warp, thin	2 ply, singles, Z, S-spun	wool, hairy medium
light tan	Persian berries	warp, thin	2 ply, singles, Z, S-spun	wool, hairy medium
black	tannin	weft, v thick	2 ply, singles, Z, S-spun	wool, hairy medium

13. Broadloom carpet, flat woven, Kidderminster type (fig. 17)

Dunn & Co., Barnard Castle, Co. Durham, 1890
Plain-weave double cloth, wool, worsted warps and wool wefts
A bordered design, the field of simple flower and leaf shapes, the inner border of two alternating flower shapes, the narrower, outer border a formal repeating pattern, in reds, brown and buff

Finished width: 8ft 9^1/2 in (268 cm)
Pattern repeat, height: 21in (53.5 cm) border and field
Overall size: 11ft 10in x 8ft 9^1/2 in (or 7ft 10in)
                          (362 x 268 cm)

Provenance: Presented to The Bowes Museum in June 1929 by Thomas Smith, who purchased the carpet in 1890 from Messrs. Dunn's Bridgegate Factory, and said to be one of the last factory-made carpets made in Barnard Castle.

This is an example of a Kidderminster broadloom carpet, developed in the 1880's and known as 'Seamless Art Squares'. The Bowes Museum has another very similar flat-woven carpet square, woven in Aspatria, Cumbria, about 1900.

The Bowes Museum accession no. 1958.1938 (carpet 14)

Technical details: Ends per inch = 28, Picks per inch = 26

Colour	Dye analysis by Dr. Taylor	Yarn Thickness	Yarn Construction	Fibre analysis/fleece type by Dr. Ryder
red	synthetic acid	warp, thin	2 ply singles, Z, S-spun	wool, hairy
brown	synthetic, mixture?	warp, thin	2 ply singles, Z, S-spun	wool, hairy
buff	tannin	warp, thin	2 ply singles, Z, S-spun	-
red	synthetic acid	weft, thick	Z-spun	wool, hairy medium, contains goat hairs
brown	synthetic mixture	weft, thick	Z-spun	wool, hairy
buff	tannin	weft, thick	Z-spun	-
tan	-	weft, thick	Z-spun	-

14. Fragment of flat-woven carpeting, possibly Dutch type

Probably Barnard Castle, Co. Durham, 19th century, second quarter.
Plain-weave single cloth, wool warps and thick wool wefts, with very small amounts of cotton and goat hair found in some yarns
Woven in warp stripes of brown, with narrow red stripes outlined in white, crossed by two double lines of thick white weft threads, to form a simple check

Pattern repeat: 4^1/2 in x 3in (11.5 x 7.5 cm)
Finished width: not known
Overall size: 14^1/4 in x 11 in x 3^1/2 in (36 x 28 x 9 cm)

Provenance: A covering for a church kneeler, under a later Brussels carpet cover, one of a number in Staindrop Church, near Barnard Castle. This church is adjacent to, and closely associated with Raby Castle. It was also refurbished in the 1840's. The recent uncovering of this piece is an exciting find as it appears to be an example of cheaper quality flat-woven carpet. The fact that it is woven in the simplest weave, using thick yarns, with small traces of hair and cotton, suggests it could be what was termed 'Dutch' carpet. Contemporary descriptions refer to Dutch as being single-ply, using lower qualities of wool or wool mixed with other fibres, in striped or chequered designs.

Lent by the Rector and Churchwardens of St. Mary's Church, Staindrop

Technical Details: Ends per inch = 18 (some working 2 as 1),
                          Picks per inch = 8
warp coloration: red, salmon pink, tan, yellow, brown
yarn thickness: medium
yarn construction: singles, S-spun
weft coloration: natural (undyed), black
yarn thickness: very thick
yarn construction: 3 ply, singles Z, S-spun

15. Fragment of Brussels carpeting from border

Possibly Barnard Castle, Co. Durham, 19th century, second quarter
Looped pile, Brussels type, worsted wool warps on jute backing
Design of intertwining ivy leaves with narrow twist border in bright pinks and greens

Pattern repeat: not known. Finished width: not known
Overall size: 4ft 0$\frac{1}{2}$ in x 20$\frac{3}{4}$ in (123 x 53cm)

Provenance: Uncatalogued item in The Bowes Museum, probably given in the 1960's by a local donor.

The Bowes Museum

This border fragment appears never to have been used. It has mitred seams and was perhaps intended to go around a hearth. Brussels was often supplied with separately woven border strips and a good example from Raby Castle is shown in plate 10. Separate borders may also have been available for Kidderminster carpeting. Some of the Barnard Castle designs, by Pratt, Son & Co., in the P.R.O. would be suitable as border patterns. An example of a flat-woven carpet with a border is in Winterthur, U.S.A. thought to be English or Scottish, 1820-40 (Montgomery, 1983, p.266).

Technical details: Ends per inch = 60, Picks per inch = 10
Pile thickness: 0.167 cm (in inches ?)
pile warp coloration: dark green, mid green, light green, dark pink, mid pink, light pink, dark yellow ochre, light ochre, yellow
warp thickness: thin, worsted
yarn construction: 2 ply, singles Z, S-spun
Backing threads of jute, both warp and weft undyed, 2 ply, singles Z, S-spun.

16. Fragment of Brussels carpeting

Possibly Barnard Castle, Co. Durham, 19th century, second quarter
Looped pile, Brussels type, Worsted wool warps on jute backing
Woven in a formal design with a medallion and stylised flowers

Pattern repeat: not known, Finished width: not known
Overall size: 13$\frac{1}{2}$ in x 20in (34.5 x 51cm)

Provenance: Found carpeting a furnished dolls' house of about 1830 in The Bowes Museum collection, given by Mrs. Frank Bell, Stubb House, Barnard Castle (see cat. no. 6)

The Bowes Museum accession no. 1940.20 (Toy 311)

Technical Details: Ends per inch = 50 pile pile thread, 10 backing threads, Picks per inch = 10 backing threads Pile thickness = 0.160
pile warp coloration: yellow, brown, orange/brown, red/brown, grey, buff, bottle green, blue grey,
warp thickness: thin, worsted
Backing threads of jute, both warp and weft, undyed.

The tapes used on the carpets

Narrow, woven fabrics with multi-coloured stripes in the warp and a single coloured weft were found on a number of the carpets. They are sewn to the underside of some of the cut edges, which were folded under and then covered by the tape, handstitched in place with linen thread. The tape prevented the edges from fraying and curling up.

Analysis of tapes on two Barnard Castle Carpets, cat no. 1 and no. 11

Single cloth structures based on a plain weave derivative
width: 1$\frac{1}{2}$ in (3.8 cm)
sett: 40 ends per inch (on average), 14 picks per inch (on average)
yarns: the warp ends combined yarns of cotton and wool. The weft yarn was made of wool

Despite the fact that these tapes would not have been visible on the face of the carpets their coloration, in both cases, complements the carpets to which they are attached. In the case of the Venetian (no.11) many of the same yarns appear to have been employed, suggesting that these braids were produced for this specific application and probably incorporated remnant yarns.

LIST OF KNOWN CARPET MANUFACTURERS

Companies by Title	Address	Earliest Date	Source
Allison J & J	Thorngate Wynd	1827	Parson & White, 1827/8
Atkin & Co		1836	Henderson, p.236
Crampton & Willis	Bridgegate	1827	Parson & White, 1827/8
Crampton, Thomas		1815	Henderson, p.236
Dunn & Ramshaw	Bridgegate	1827	Parson & White, 1827/8
Dunn, Richard	Bridgegate	1847	White, 1847
Harrison, Crosby, Dunn		1824	Richardson, MA 1843
Hepworth, Joseph (Partner of Dunn)		1858	Will of R Dunn 1871
London Carpet Co	Bridgegate	1867	*Teesdale Mercury* 24/7/1867
Monkhouse, Dixon, Whitfield	Thorngate	1828	Pigot, 1827/8
Monkhouse, Whitfield & Co	The Bank	1834	Pigot, 1834
Monkhouse, Joshua & Sons		1840	Company bill-head
Monkhouse Brothers	Thorngate	1854	Slater 1854
Pratt, Son & Co	Bridgegate	1848	Slater 1848
Raine, Edward Son & Co	Bridgegate	1834	Pigot 1834
Smith & Co		1878	*Teesdale Mercury* 18/12/1878
Smith & Powell	Bridgegate	1867	*Teesdale Mercury* 30/1/1867
Smith Bros	Bridgegate	1876	Slater 1876/7
Winskill, Atkin & Co	Bridgegate	1834	Pigot 1834
Winskill, Mr. J		1836	Henderson, p.236
Winskill, John		1836	Henderson, p.236
Winskill, Jordan & Hildreth		1827	Parson & White 1827

Other Individuals

Appleby John		1883	Baptism Reg. 27/12/1833
Dodd Richard	Thorngate	1834	Pigot 1834
Ellary Thomas	Bridgegate	1841	Census 1841
Peacock, George		1840	Baptism Reg. 27/5/1840

DESIGNS REGISTERED IN THE PUBLIC RECORD OFFICE

Registered designs for carpets, from firms in Barnard Castle, 1842 to 1853, in The Public Record Office, Kew

These designs are numbered in the P.R.O. volumes in a single sequence, according to the date received and not by manufacturer. The numbers stamped on the designs do not relate to pattern numbers used within individual firms.

Dimensions are for whole paper. Most carry a 1-2 cm border on at least two sides, of unprinted paper, often with a printed stationers inscription. Few show full repeat of design.

Volume BT.43.105

Page 13

No. 1740 Pratt, Son & Co., Barnard Castle (27 Sept 1842) No. 1002. Squared paper (16 to inch). Design in red. Formal damask-like scrolls with border of close, upward growing 'urns' (approx 7cm). Inscribed on border: '1740 - No. 1002. Pratt Son & Co. Barnard Castle'. H: 9 cm, W: 18.5 cm.

No. 1741 Pratt, Son & Co., Barnard Castle (27 Sept 1842) Squared paper (16 to inch). Design in red, formal, borders (2 squares approx 9 cm). Inscribed in ink on border: 'No. 1000'. H: 11 cm, W: 20 cm.

No. 1742 Pratt, Son & Co., Barnard Castle (27 Sept 1842) Squared paper (16 to inch). Design in red. Two small motifs (2 squares approx 8 cm square). Inscribed on plain borders: 'No. 1001'. H: 9 cm, W: 19 cm.

Page 49

No. 2540 Pratt, Son & Co., Barnard Castle (1 Dec 1842) **fig. 18** Squared paper (16 to inch). Design in red. Border (about 7 cm) of interlinked ovals. Body geometric (elongated crosses and octagons). Border reads 'POINT PAP' H: 8 cm, W: 18 cm.

No. 2541 Pratt, Son & Co., Barnard Castle (1 Dec 1842) **fig. 19** Squared paper (16 to inch). Design in red. Greek key border (7 cm). Body of large-scale seaweed design. H: 17 cm, W: 14 cm.

No. 2542 Pratt, Son & Co., Barnard Castle (1 Dec 1842) **fig. 20** Squared paper (16 to inch). Design in red. Border (7 cm) of linked rectangles. Body of strapwork. Inscribed in ink on plain border: 'No. 1005'. H: 18 cm, W: 13 cm.

Volume BT.43.106

Page 259

No. 16170 Pratt, Son & Co., Barnard Castle (13 Feb 1844) **fig. 22** Squared paper (16 to inch). Design in scarlet. Very large scale scrolling design with heart's-ease-like leaves. H: 43 cm, W: 75 cm approx.

Page 289

No. 17268 Pratt, Son & Co., Barnard Castle (21 Mar 1844) Squared paper (16 to inch). Design in bright red. Border of scrolling, feather-like leaves approx 7 cm. Body of looser arabesques of rose-heads and leaves. H: 13 cm, W: 16.5 cm.

Page 307

No. 18146 Pratt, Son & Co., Barnard Castle (2 May 1844) **fig. 21** Squared paper (16 to inch). Bright red design. Integral border (approx 9 cm) tightly scrolling acanthus. Body of loose sprigs, flowers and hart's-tongue fern. H: 13 cm, W: 18 cm.

Page 316

No. 18282 Pratt, Son & Co., Barnard Castle (15 May 1844) Squared paper (16 to inch). Bright red design. 7 cm integral border of scrolling anthemia (formalised honeysuckle motifs). Body of loose rose-like flower-heads. H: 10 cm, W: 16.5 cm.

Volume BT. 43. 107

Page 357

No. 19895 Pratt, Son & Co., Barnard Castle (7 July 1844)
Squared paper (16 to inch). Design in red. Border (9 cm) of alternate diagonal 'bricks' (4 deep) with formal flower-head motifs. Centre appears to be damask-like. H: 17 cm, W: 13 cm.

No. 19896 Pratt, Son & Co., Barnard Castle (7 July 1844)
Squared paper (16 to inch). Design in red. Formal scroll design, a border of slightly heavier upright motifs (6 cm). H: 17 cm, W: 15 cm.

No. 21893 Pratt, Son & Co., Barnard Castle (27 Sept 1844)
Squared paper (16 to inch). Design in red. Large design of formal scrolls. Border (6.5 cm) of lunettes filled with tight scrolls. H: 17 cm, W: 20 cm.

Volume BT.43.108

No. 27503 Monkhouse, Whitfield & Co., Barnard Castle (13 May 1845) **plate 12**
Squared paper (16 to inch). Polychrome design of Greek fret, minarets and flowers. Approx. H: 58 cm, W: 38 cm. Paper printed on margins: 'R. Hay & Son, successor to A Blaikie, Paisley'.

No. 29753 Pratt, Son & Co., Barnard Castle (14 Aug 1845) **fig. 23**
Squared paper (16 to inch). Design in red. Large tiled-floor design with some semi-formal flowers. H: 22 cm, W: 22 cm.

Volume BT.43.114

No. 80130 Richard Dunn, Barnard Castle (9 Aug 1851) **plate 13**
Squared paper (12 to inch - but divided into heavy squares every 6th square). Design in crimson and cream on maroon ground. Border (7 cm) of crimson curled leaves on maroon, ground of cream seaweed on same ground. One plain border, printed: '50 x 40 Designs' '8 by 6 No. 1'. Inscribed in ink on border: 'Richard Dunn Carpet Manufacturer, Barnard Castle No. 348. H: 14.5 cm, W: 15.5 cm.

Volume BT.43.115

No. 91996 Richard Dunn, Barnard Castle (5 Aug 1853)
Squared paper (16 to inch). Design in browny-red. Border (8 cm) with growing stem with rose-like flowers (stepped outer border). Body close carpeted with formal oriental carpet motifs including birds. Top plain border inscribed in ink: 'Richard Dunn Carpet Manufacturer Barnard Castle Yorkshire'. No. 392' 'class 6'. H: 24 cm, W: 16 cm.

The kinds of wool used in the manufacture of the carpets
Michael L. Ryder

Introduction

A fundamental feature of any textile, which is often ignored, is the nature of the fibre used in its construction. With wool textiles this means the kind of fleece used. Although there are hundreds of sheep breeds throughout the world, there are only about six main types of fleece (Ryder, 1983; 1987a). By measuring the diameter of fibres in a sample of yarn it is possible to define the type of fleece, but it is not usually possible to identify the breed of sheep from which the wool has come. The hairy fleeces of British hill breeds with a black face are usually described as carpet wools, whereas in fact in modern carpet manufacture such fleeces provide only one of several types used in a 'blend' (mixture) to produce the desired characteristics at an acceptable price. Other fleece types in the blend might be the less-hairy wools of medium fibre diameter. Such wools wear better than hairy wools, and fibre measurement has shown that this was the main type used in old oriental carpets (Ryder, 1987b). Investigation of The Bowes Museum carpets indicates that the wool they were made from included some very hairy examples of the Hairy fleece type, with some hairy examples of the Medium fleece type and\the suggestion that some of the yarns might have been a blend of Hairy and Medium wools.

Materials and Methods

Several warp and several weft yarns from eight carpets were sampled and measured. The results are shown in the catalogue of carpets.

Gross and General Textile Observations

In general the warp yarns were thinner and more tightly spun than the weft yarns, the warps being 1mm or less, while the wefts ranged from 1mm to 2mm in thickness, except the Venetians (Cat nos 11 & 12) which had wefts of 4 to 5mm. These are not precise yarn measurements but approximate values to give an indication of the thickness. Many of the warps seem to have been worsted-spun (and it is of interest that Jacob Allison's supplies included worsted yarn). The warps usually had a Z spinning twist and were often S-plied, while the wefts were woollen spun with an S twist. Although dye analysis was not part of this investigation, certain features observed under the microscope are worthy of note. The dye tended to be denser on the outside than on the inside of the yarns, which supports the conclusion that they were yarn-dyed and that the wool had not been dyed before spinning. This also means that any blending of different fleece types was carried out before dyeing. However the pink warp of cat no. 11 had many fibres lacking dye, which could indicate mixing after dyeing.

Microscopic Measurements of the Fibres

All the wools used were hairy; the percentage of medullated (hollow) fibres ranged from 3% to over 40% which is less than the amount of medullation in the hairiest Scottish Blackface sheep today (Ryder, 1985). About half the wools had no natural pigment at all and amongst those with pigmented fibres the incidence was small.

The overall fibre diameter range was from individual underwool fibres as fine as 10 microns (1 micron = 0.001mm) to outer coat hairs as coarse as 180 microns. Hairy fibres so coarse are unusual in sheep, in which the upper limit is about 100 microns. Although most of these were quite clearly from sheep, a few of the coarsest hairs appeared to have the characteristics of goat hair, which raises the possibility that some of the wools might have been blended with goat hair. Although some of the wools were of modern true Hairy (H) fleece type as found in the Scottish Blackface and Swaledale breeds, others with a less coarse upper limit (60 - 80 microns) might have been of more primitive Hairy-medium (HM) fleece type as found in the Cheviot and Welsh Mountain breeds.

The elimination of hairy fibres from the Hairy-medium type by selective breeding during prehistory produced the modern true Medium fleece type (M) which has a symmetrical fibre diameter distribution in which the mean value is not very different from the mode (the most frequent value)(Ryder, 1983). The coarser fibres of this type are the non-hairy fibres sought by carpet manufacturers. Such fleeces are found in certain Down breeds and in particular the Longwools, about 10 per cent of which might be included in a modern carpet wool blend. More recently among old wools and some primitive breeds a Medium fleece type has been discovered which also has hairy fibres. This has been designated hairy Medium (hyM) and some of the Bowes yarns were clearly this type.

Thus in carpets Cat Nos 3 and 8, while some yarns were clearly of Hairy (H) fleece types, others were of hairy Medium (hyM) fleece type. The wools in carpets Cat nos 1 and 13 were less easy to interpret since although basically hairy, they had a greater proportion of medium fibres than expected. They appear to be Hairy fleeces with which Medium (and most likely hairy Medium) fleeces had been blended. This possible evidence for the mixing of different types of wool prior to processing warrants further investigation.

Discussion

Most of the suppliers of wool (in the form of yarn) listed in the account books of Jacob Allison studied by Jean Hemingway were within a radius of 50 miles and it is tempting to suggest that the Hairy wools came from the local black-faced Swaledale breed, while the Medium and hairy Medium wools came from the long-woolled Teeswater. But 'Scotch wool' is listed and other suppliers were located in the West Riding and as far afield as London, so further analysis of yarns and the records would be required to link the type of fleece observed with its possible source.

References

Ryder, M. L. (1983) *Sheep and Man* (Duckworth, London)

Ryder, M. L. (1985) 'Cross-breeding studies with selected fleece lines of Scottish Blackface sheep', *J. Textile Inst.* 76, 362-276.

Ryder, M. L. (1987a) 'Evolution of the fleece' *Scientific American*, 155, 112-19.

Ryder, M. L. (1987b) 'The Measurement of Wool Fibres and Yarns as an Aid to Defining Carpet Type', *Oriental Carpet and Textile Studies*, III, 134-53.

APPENDIX II

Dye Analysis of carpet samples.
Dr. G. W. Taylor

Experimental

The samples of coloured yarns from eight carpets received from The Bowes Museum were subjected to the natural dye test sequence (Walton and Taylor, 1991) and also to solvent fastness tests as appropriate (Schweppe, 1979). Natural dyes were identified by means of spectrophotometry and thin layer chromatography (TLC). Synthetic dyes were classified by type but not individually identified.

Results

The samples and test results are included in the catalogue of carpets. The blue dye on many of the carpets was found to be Saxe blue. Invented in 1740, this dye was very popular in the 19th century. It was made by treating natural indigo with sulphuric acid.

A deep black could be obtained by use of logwood (Haematoxylon ampechianum L.) with iron mordant. Other blacks were made using tannin (from woody materials) with iron mordant. Tannin could also be used, perhaps with iron mordant, as a yellow or brown tinting agent.

Tannin may also be the identifiable residue of a natural dye of woody origin where other components of the dye have decayed.

Two natural yellow colorants can be confidently identified as luteolin and quercetin . Luteolin is the main colorant in weld (Reseda luteola L.) and dyers greenweed (Genista tinctoria L). Both are possibilities in the present context, weld being perhaps the more likely. Quercetin is the colorant in quercitron bark, introduced from America in the 1790s, and it is interesting to find an example of such a dyeing in Cat. No. 7. Other natural yellow mordant dyes, where the identifications are probable, but not certain, are Persian berries (the unripe fruit of plants of the buckthorn group) and old fustic (Chlorophora tinctoria Gard.). In a number of cases, natural yellow mordant dyes were indicated by TLC, but it was not possible to identify the dyes because of the very small amounts present.

The soluble redwoods are a group of dyewoods which all contain the same colorant. brasilein. Perhaps the best known of this group are brazilwood and sappanwood. Sappanwood was imported from the east. Examples of soluble redwood dyeings are found in carpets Cat. Nos 7 and 12. The different tints found are probably the result of different mordant combinations, the presence of more or less tannin, and variable degrees of fading (soluble redwood dyeings are fugitive to light).

The most widely used natural red dye at this time was cochineal, which gives a purplish red with alum and a scarlet with tin mordant.

Synthetic dyes have been detected on three carpets. They are classified as synthetic for two reasons; (i) their spectra in various solvents are not in accord with those of known natural dyes; and (ii) their lack of fastness to a range of solvents, in particular in the present case their tendency to be fugitive in water, which is not characteristic of natural dyeings.

Discussion

The first synthetic dyes came into use in the 1860s. Cat. No. 3 must, then be later than the suggested date of the second quarter of the 19th century, though it is interesting (but by no means unusual) that all the dyes other than the red appear to be natural. Similarly, Cat. No. 11 cannot be as early as the suggested date of 1844; though its figured companion Cat. No.12 could certainly be from that time, all its dyes being natural.

With regard to the other carpets, the results on Cat. No. 1 are perfectly in accord with a date in the second quarter of the 19th century, and Cat. No. 8 may well be from the mid-century. Cat. No. 2. also contains dyes compatible with a date from the latter part of the 18th century to about one hundred years later. The presence of synthetic dyes in Cat. No. 13 allows a date of 1890, though the finding of tannin suggests a natural source for the buff colour.

References

Schweppe, H., 1979. 'Identification of dyes on old textiles', *Journal of the American Institute for Conservation*, 19/1 (Fall 1979), 14-23

Walton, P., and Taylor, G., 1991. 'The characterisation of dyes in textiles from archaeological excavations', *Chromatography and Analysis*, 17, 5-7.

Note: by Jean Hemingway

When the information above is compared with that available from Jacob Allison's books (Chapter 7) the following points arise:-

a) Nearly all the dyes found by Taylor were used by Allison. Exceptions are Persian berries and dyer's greenweed, but Allison had several other sources of yellow colouring.

b) Allison used dyestuffs not existing in the Taylor study: peachwood: barwood: inca (or incu): bark: and cochineal in the forms of grain tin and lac dye.

c) Taylor suggests mordants: iron, sulphuric acid, alum and tin. Allison certainly bought oil of vitriol (sulphuric acid) and used urine, which contains alum. He purchased vitriol, which may include any of the metallic compounds copper sulphate, iron sulphate and zinc sulphate, as these were sometimes generally known as vitriol. He bought two potassium compounds, cream of tartar and argol. He also bought spirits of salts, (hydrochloric acid).

GLOSSARY

Angola carpet

Appears in a bill from Joshua Monkhouse & Sons, dated 1849 (fig.9) and refers to a type of presumably flat-woven carpeting, a cheaper quality than figured Venetian and probably single ply. Name presumably derived from angola yarn, a mixture of wool and cotton and other fibre. Angola fabric was a woven imitation of the cashmere shawl in the early 19th century, which contained angora goat hair. The term Angola was originally derived from Angora.

Broad powerloom

Developed in the early 1880's for Kidderminster carpets, to produce seamless carpeting made 2 yards or more in width, known as 'Art Squares'.

Brussels carpet

A type of strip carpeting with a pile of uncut loops. The loops are formed by supplementary worsted warps going over rods, which are inserted and then withdrawn as the weaving progresses. A binding warp and weft of linen thread provides a backing.

Camblets (camlet)

A worsted wool fabric used for dress and furnishings. Made in England in the early seventeenth century. Could be mixed with goat's hair, silk or linen.

Crape

A light fabric of worsted and silk used for mourning

Cumber (comber)

A term referring to the pattern repeat in Kidderminster and Brussels carpeting in which one pattern extended across the breadth of the carpet. Name possibly derived from comber board, the board on a loom containing rows of holes for each harness cord that determine the height, width and spacing of the cards in jacquard weaving. Monkhouses advertised 'cumber and point styles' in the Great Exhibition Catalogue, 1851 (fig.11). It was an intricate and complicated way of producing a pattern, requiring twice as many harness cords as for 'point' designs.

Diaper pattern

A weave pattern with lines crossing to form diamonds with the spaces variously filled with lines, a dot or a figure of some kind - originally applied to linen fabric.

Double cloth

A reversible compound fabric in which the two cloths are woven so as to interchange with each other. The pattern created is the same on both faces of the cloth, but the colours are reversed. The technique was known in Europe in the seventeenth century but it is not known if it was used for carpeting before the 1730s. A patent of 1825 described the double cloth technique as 'the manner in which Kidderminster, Yorkshire or Scotch carpeting have always been wove'. Also called two-ply.

Draw-loom

A hand loom for patterned fabrics, with a special type of figure harness to control the warp ends. To create the pattern, it was necessary to lift the appropriate warp ends in the loom for insertion of the weft. This was done by the draw-boy pulling the lashes (loops) which were attached to the cords of the harness to lift the warp ends, which could be selected individually or in repeat groups.

Drawing in

The process of drawing the thread of the warp through the eyes of the heddles.

Dutch carpet

The simplest and cheapest type of flat-woven strip carpeting, woven in single-ply, it was little more than a thick woollen cloth and not hard-wearing. The woollen yarns were often mixed with cotton and other fibres such as goat hair. Monkhouses advertised 'Dutch fabric carpets, warp made from silk noils' in 1851 (fig. 11).

Ends (and picks)

The warp threads of a woven cloth (picks are the weft threads). The spacing of the ends and picks, expressed as threads per inch is called the sett.

Flat-woven (carpet)

A type of carpeting woven without a pile, literally a floor-cloth. A heavy woollen fabric suitable for use on the floor could have been produced anywhere where worsted yarn was available.

Hairy Fibre

Coarse fibre originating from the outer coat of the wild ancestor of the sheep, having a hollow central core (medulla). Divided into kemps and hairs.

Hairy Fleece

Modern fleece type with skewed/continuous fibre diameter distribution ranging from fine to medium wool fibres through hairs to kemps.

Hairy-Medium fleece

The second most primitive fleece type, which first appeared in the Bronze Age, having fine kemps, medium fibres and fine wool fibres. The fibre diameter distribution is skewed so that most of the ribres are fine and theire is a 'tail' of coarser fibres.

Heddle (heald)

A looped card, shaped wire or steel strip with an eye in the centre, through which a warp yarn is threaded so that its movement may be controlled during weaving.

Ingrain

The common name in the U.S.A. for the flat-woven strip carpeting also called Kidderminster or Scotch. Name derived from the fact that the yarn was dyed before weaving, not dyed in the piece.

Jacquard loom

Invented by Joseph Marie Jacquard (1752-1834) about 1801. It was an attachment to a loom, not an actual loom, which employed wire needles and a series of punched cards which mechanically selected the warp threads and raised them when necessary. The drawboy, who had previously manipulated the warp cords for the weaver, was no longer needed.

Kemp

Short, bristly, very coarse and chalky white fibre with very wide latticed medulla. Can range up to 150 microns.

Kersey

A cheap, coarse, woollen cloth of twill weave, a traditional product of Yorkshire woollen manufacture.

Kidderminster carpet

A general name given to double and triplecloth strip-carpeting named after the town in Worcestershire where it was first reputedly made from about 1735. So named probably because the industry was formally organised in Kidderminster at this early date, rather than because this type of fabric was peculiar to that town.

Medium fleece

Modern fleece type with a symmetrical fibre diameter distribution in which the mode (most frequent diameter) and mean are about 35 microns.

Micron

The unit used to measure fibre diameter = 0.001mm.

Mordants

Substances which, partly or wholly, combine with the dyestuff to form definite compounds in the fibre; the colour obtained is dependent both on the mordant and the dyestuff.

Noils

The shorter fibres, separated from the longer fibres in combing, usually applied to wool, but also applied to silk. An inferior quality and therefore cheaper.

Picks (and ends)

The weft threads of a woven cloth (ends are the warp threads). The spacing of the ends and picks, expressed as threads per inch, is called the sett.

Plain weave

The simplest of all weaves, in which each weft (pick) passes over and then under each warp (end).

Point

Also known as 'mirror repeat', where the pattern is repeated from the centre to the sides, as in 'point styles' used to describe Monkhouse's goods displayed at the Great Exhibition of 1851 (fig. 11).

Satin weave

A warp faced weave producing a smooth cloth surface, free from twill (diagonal lines).

Scotch Carpet

Flat-woven strip carpeting made in Scotland from the middle of the 18th century. Strips were usually one Scottish ell (37 inches, 0.94 cm wide). From 1824, triplecloth as well as double cloth was woven. During the 19th century the term Scotch became synonymous with Kidderminster and Ingrain carpeting and did not necessarily indicate the place of origin.

Shags

An eighteenth century term for a heavy, worsted fabric with a long nap (raised fibrous surface).

Singles

A thread produced by one unit of a spinning machine.

Slay or sley

A weaver's reed used for separating warp threads.

Spun - S spun, Z spun

Fibres are spun to produce a continuous thread and the spiral direction of the twist is indicated either by the letter S (clock wise) or Z (anti-clockwise).

Tammies

Strong, lightweight worsted of plain weave and open texture, often glazed.

Tapestry carpet

A pile carpet in which the pile warp was printed before being attached to the loom. It was a cheap imitation of Brussels and Wilton. Known as Tapestry Brussels (looped pile) and Tapestry Velvet (cut pile). Brussels and Wilton were restricted to 5 or 6 colours and each colour had a set of pile warps. Tapestry carpet had just one set, printed with an unlimited number of colours. It was therefore more economical, using less wool. The printing mechanism, on rollers, was patented by Richard Whytock of Edinburgh in 1832.

Tow yarns

Low-grade linen thread made of short fibres.

Triple cloth or three-ply

Woven in the same manner as double cloth, but with three interchanging cloths. In 1812 Thomas Lea of Kidderminster obtained a patent for weaving Kidderminster or Scotch carpet, with three or more warps, i.e. with three layers of cloth, adding bulk and the possibility of more colours. Sometimes referred to as Imperial Kidderminster.

Twill weave

Produces diagonal lines on the face of the cloth.

Venetian carpet

A type of flat-woven strip carpeting, generally striped, and often made in narrower widths (22in or 27in) for corridors and stairs. It was a warp-faced weave, in which the warp carried the design and the weft threads, normally a thick black yarn, were not visible. The term Venetian is applied to fabrics with a warp-faced satin weave, and may have originated in Venice. Figured Venetians had more elaborate patterning than a stripe, woven in a warp twill. According to Ure's Dictionary they were woven on two-ply Kidderminster looms, not the simple looms used for ordinary Venetian. In fig. 42 both 'Figured and Venetian Looms' are advertised.

Wilton

A form of strip carpeting with a pile, woven like Brussels but the looped pile is cut to form a 'velvet' pile. The loops are cut during the weaving process by a blade on the rods which form the loops when they are withdrawn.

Wool Fibre

Fibre originating from the underwool of the wild ancestor of the sheep; can be Fine (20 microns) or Medium (40 mircons).

Worsted

Yarn of long-stapled wool which has been combed to produce a smoother, stronger yarn than woollen yarn which is softer, spun from shorter wool fibres.

Main References used in Glossary

Burnham, D.K. *A Textile Terminology: Warp & Weft*, (London 1981)

Hefford, W. 'Patents for strip-carpets, 1741-1851' *Furniture History Vol. XXIII*, 1987 1-8,

Montgomery, F, *Textiles in America 1650-1870*, (New York, 1983)

The Textile Institute, *Textile Terms and Definitions*, (Manchester, 1975)

and contemporary accounts e.g. *Penny Cyclopedia*, Ure's Dictionary (see Bibliography).

The definitions of fleece types were provided by Dr. M.L. Ryder.

Selected Bibliography

Primary Sources

Allison, Jacob, (1795-1868) Accounts 1823-1852 (copy in The Bowes Museum)

Admissions Register, Barnard Castle Infants School 1862-1883, 1887-1958 (Durham County Council)

Brown, G., *Report to Teesdale Poor Law Union Barnard Castle, 1837* (Public Record Office)

Census Returns 1841-91, (Darlington Public Library)

Cotherstone Quaker Meeting Minutes, 1785-1837 (Durham County Record Office)

Hanby-Holmes Papers, (Durham County Record Office)

Minutes of Barnard Castle open and select vestry 1726-1963 (Durham County Record Office)

Probate Records (Principal Probate Registry, London; University of York, Borthwick Institute; University of Durham, Department of Paleography)

Smith, L.D.   *The Carpet weavers of Kidderminster* PhD. unpublished thesis (Birmingham University, 1982)

Newspapers

The *Darlington and Stockton Times*, Darlington, 1847 onwards

The *Teesdale Mercury*, Barnard Castle, 1854 onwards

Supplement to *Teesdale Mercury: Century of Local Government* 26.7.1950

Directories

Baines, E,   *Directory of ... North Riding of Yorkshire* (London, 1822)

Kelly & Co   *Post Office Directory of Northumberland & Durham* (London, 1858)

Parson, W. & White, W.   *Directory of .... Durham & Northumberland* Vol. 1, (Leeds, 1827)

Pigot, J.   *Directory of ... Cumberland, Durham, Northumberland, Westmorland and Yorkshire* (London & Manchester, 1828)

Pigot, J.   *Directory of ... Durham, Northumberland and Yorkshire* (London & Manchester, 1834)

Pigot, J.   *London Directory* (London, 1839)

White, F.   *Directory of ... Tyne, Wear and Tees* (Sheffield, 1847)

Whellan, W.   *Directory of ... Durham* (London and Manchester, 1894)

Secondary Sources

Austin, D. and Tallentire, W.L.   Barnard Castle. First interim report: excavations in the town ward 1974-76; *Journal of the British Archaeological Association, Vol. CXXII* (1979)

Bartlett, J.N.   *Carpeting the Millions: the growth of Britain's carpet industry* (Edinburgh, 1978)

Beaumont, R.   *Woollen and Worsted Cloth Manufacture* (London, 1888)

Bradbury, F.   *Calculations in Yarns and Fabrics* (Halifax, n.d., about 1930)

Bradbury, F.   *Carpet Manufacture, Belfast,* (London & Boston, Mass., 1904)

Brayby, E.W & Britton J.   *Beauties of England and Wales,* (London, 1820) Vol. V

Brewster, J.   *Parochial History and Antiquities of Stockton on Tees* (Stockton on Tees, 1829) 2nd edition (facsimile Stockton on Tees, 1971)

Brinton, R.S.   *Carpets,* (Common commodities & industries series) (London, 1939)

Ellis, A.   *Three Hundred Years of London River: the Hay's Wharf Story* (London, 1952)

Fordyce, W.   *History ... of Durham* (Newcastle, 1856) Vol. II

Garland, R.   *A Tour in Teesdale* (York, 1828)

Garland, R.   *A Tour in Teesdale* (York, 1834)

Gilbert, C.,   *Country House Floors Temple Newsam Country*
I. Lomax, &   *House studies* No. 3, (Leeds: City Art Galleries, 1987)
A. Wells-Cole

Great Exhibition   *Official Descriptive and Illustrated catalogue 1851,*
                   (London, 1851) Vol. II

Hefford, W.   'Patents for strip carpeting 1741-1851', *Furniture History*
                   Vol. XXIII, (1987) 1-8

Hemingway, J.   'Jacob Allison; carpet manufacturer', *Textile History*
                   Vol 27, No. 2 (1996)

Henderson, W.   'On the Manufacture of Carpeting', in *The Industrial
                   Resources of the three Northern Rivers, the Tyne, Wear
                   and Tees, including the reports on the Local Manufactures,
                   read before the British Association 1863,* ed. W.G.
                   Armstrong, I.L. Bell, J. Taylor and Dr. Richardson, 2nd
                   edition, (London and Newcastle, 1864)

Hutchinson, W.   *An Excursion to the Lakes* (London, 1776)

Hutchinson, W.   *History .... of Durham* (Carlisle, 1794)

Hutton, W.   *The State We're In* (London, 1995)

Kapelle, W.E.   *The Norman Conquest of the North* (London, 1979)

Kraak, D.   'Carpets', *The Magazine Antiques, Vol. CXLIX,* (Jan.
                   1996) 184-91

Lanier, M.   *English and Oriental Carpets at Williamsburg*
                   (Charlottesville, 1975)

Layton, G.   *Castle Barnard - a poem* (Barnard Castle, 1823)

Montgomery, F.   *Textiles in America 1650-1870* (New York, 1984)

Mackenzie   *History ... of Durham,* (Newcastle upon Tyne, 1834)
& Ross

Ranger, W.   *Report to the General Board of Health* (H.M.S.O.1850)
                   (copy in The Bowes Museum)

Richardson, M.A.   *Local Historian's Table Book of Remarkable Occurrences*
                   (Newcastle, 1843), Vol. III

Rock & Co   *Views & Scenery of Barnard Castle* (London, about 1875)

Shea, W.   *Carpet Making in Durham City* (Durham, 1984)

Sherrill, S.   *Carpets and Rugs of Europe and America* (New York,
                   1996)

Smith, L.D.   'Industrial organisation in the Kidderminster carpet
                   trade', *Textile History,* Vol. 14, (1984) 75-100

Society for the Diffusion of Useful Knowledge

                   The Penny Cyclopaedia, Vol. VI (London, 1836)

                   'A day at the Scotch carpet factory' *The Penny
                   Magazine,* New Series, part *XXXII* (London, 1843) 329-
                   336

Spencer, H.   *Local Records of South Durham 1819-1827* (Darlington,
                   1866)

Swain, M.   'A note on Scotch carpets' *Furniture History XIV,* (1978)
                   61-62

Topham, E.   *Letters from Edinburgh,* London, 1776, XXI

Ure, A.   *Dictionary of Arts, Manufacturers and Mines* (London,
                   1839) Vol. 1, (7th edition 1878)

Watson, J.   *The Theory and Practice of the Art of Weaving by Hand
                   and Power* (Glasgow, 1863)

Webster, E.   *Textiles and Tools* (Halifax, 1970)

Whittock, N. et al.

                   The Complete Book of Trades (1837)

Young, A.   *A Six Month's Tour through the North of England* (London,
                   1770) Vol II